Intelligent Tennis

A Sensible Approach To Playing Your Best Tennis... Consistently.

**Skip Singleton,
USPTA Professional**

Foreword by Ken Rosewall

BETTERWAY PUBLICATIONS, INC.
WHITE HALL, VIRGINIA

Published by Betterway Publications, Inc.
Box 219
Crozet, VA 22932

Cover design by Deborah B. Chappell
Cover painting © LeRoy Neiman
Typography by East Coast Typography, Inc.

8/94

Library of Congress Cataloging-in-Publication Data

Singleton, Skip
  Intelligent tennis.

  Includes index.
  1. Tennis—Psychological aspects.   I. Title.
GV1002.9.P75S57   1988   796.342′01′9   88–19346
ISBN 1-55870-102-8 (pbk.)

Printed in the United States of America
9 8 7 6 5 4 3

*This book is dedicated to the most
supportive person I've ever known,
my first editor, typist and best friend . . .
my wife, Debbie.*

♕ *ACKNOWLEDGMENTS*

I would like to thank the many fine professionals, players, and students I've been fortunate enough to be associated with over the years. They've given to me so much out of life! Thanks also to Bob and Jackie Hostage at BETTERWAY PUBLICATIONS for their constant belief and enthusiasm for this book.

The author, Skip Singleton (on left) and Ken Rosewall discussing
Intelligent Tennis.

♀ *FOREWORD*

Tennis has been very good to me, through my growing up years and through all of my adult life. It continues to afford me the chance to play competitively — keeping things in perspective — on the Grand Masters Tour. It was the tour that took me to the Bluewater Bay Resort in Niceville, Florida, where I had the pleasure of meeting the Tennis Director, Skip Singleton.

I got to know Skip quite well during my stay at Bluewater Bay. It became clear very quickly that he sees tennis as a game for a lifetime. As a certified teaching professional, Skip imparts his knowledge of the game and his enthusiasm for it to players of all ages, at all skill levels. And while he instructs them in all the physical aspects of the game — serving, ground strokes, footwork, etc. — he acquaints them early with the mental aspects of the game; non-physical skills any player needs to play "intelligent tennis" to the best of his or her ability. His book focuses principally on those mental skills — analysis, motivation, inspiration, and self-discipline.

It is no secret that tennis has changed in many respects since I won my first tournament in 1952. The ability, time, and energy that Skip has devoted to writing this book will benefit tennis enthusiasts of all ages, at all levels of play. I believe they will enjoy it as much as I have.

Ken Rosewall

Contents

♀ INTRODUCTION

Everyone has the capability to play up to their potential, that is, to play their best tennis. The question is, why do so few players do it?

The top players in the game, the true champions, seem to consistently play their best. They make it into the finals of the major tennis events year after year. These players seem to possess a unique understanding of the game and of themselves. But these same players also make mistakes with their play and have experienced failures. So what makes them different? How are they able to overcome their defeats and perform well consistently over the years? They have all learned to play the game *intelligently*. They have the proper attitude and determination to learn from their mistakes and go forward. They know their limitations and play their games within them. In doing so, they have become masters of the sport.

To most, mastering the game of tennis would seem almost impossible. Goals are consequently set much lower, and therefore self-esteem. These players will play the game in awe of it, never really understanding the true basics of the game or how to improve their own play. Tennis often becomes a struggle with inconsistent performance for them. They will play the game until they are advanced in years, experienced in ability, or wise enough to try to develop some kind of understanding for this complex game.

To play well consistently doesn't have to be such a struggle. Tennis can become much easier to master when you learn to utilize all of your resources. Most people will realize only about one percent of their mental potential. They have a computerized mind that will remain mostly in the "off" position. Consistently winning players have learned to turn their minds "on" — their mental capabilities help them realize their potential. They use their minds to control their thoughts, especially those of belief and confidence in themselves. They also use their minds to foster a winning attitude and to focus attention on the task. These players usually establish who they are by being in control of the ball, of themselves, of their opponent, and of the match. They tend to dominate their opponents, some of whom might have superior tennis skills compared to their own.

15

This book was written to show how everyone can perform well by learning to play an intelligent game of tennis. It is within your grasp; it will simply take a commitment on your part to develop and practice the principles discussed in this book. Reread it often to keep the good habits fresh in your mind.

Some advanced tournament players may want to omit reading Chapter 1 as this covers the basics of the game of tennis. Others may feel the need to read this chapter for a good refresher course. In any event, Chapter 1 is important because your tennis game will not progress without a good working knowledge of the basics.

Best of luck with your tennis game and I hope that you discover how enjoyable tennis can be when you learn to play intelligently. What a joy it will be never to experience the agony of beating yourself again!

CHAPTER 1

Understanding the Basics

☖ *TENNIS: A FASCINATING GAME*

The game of tennis in most players' eyes is one of *fascination.* It is a fascinating game because of the sensational styles of the champions who play the game of tennis. Players like Gabriela Sabatini with her heavy topspin and two-handed backhand, John McEnroe with his artistic touch, Boris Becker with his pounding serve, and Steffi Graff with her awesome forehand. These are all fascinating players to watch.

To truly understand how they play the game, you must first get beyond this realm of fascination. You must take a deeper look into what the game is all about to develop a better understanding of it. To learn to play this game, you must first learn *how* to correctly play it.

Is there any one way to play tennis correctly? Many coaches and players have tried to sell a magic formula for "the way to play the game." This book does not contain such a special system. Instead, it will help you understand more about the game and about yourself, so that you will have the necessary knowledge to play the game you desire. It is important to first learn the basics of the game because it is upon these that your game will be built. Without a clear understanding of them, you will never develop the necessary self-confidence in your ability to reach your potential best.

What is it that most people build their games on when they are unsure of the basics? *Fascination.* They attempt to hit hard, low shots like Connors, try a testy temperament like McEnroe, or even change to a new diet like Navratilova. They might take a series of lessons from their tennis professional to improve their game or attempt some new technique they've read about in a tennis magazine. Yet they will probably remain uncomfortable with their play. To develop your game you must first have a solid foundation to build upon. This solid foundation is called "The Basics."

♀ BALL CONTROL, THE MOST MISUNDERSTOOD BASIC

A tennis ball will only travel in the direction in which you direct it with your stroke! If you are hitting a ball in the wrong direction and are unsure why this is occurring, what is lacking is knowledge of how to control the ball. The ball goes where it does on every hit for a *reason*. Your understanding of this reason is the initial step in learning how to play a controlled game of tennis.

All shots in tennis should be hit with a *target* in mind. By deliberately directing the ball on each stroke at a target, you create control over where the ball is placed. This ability to control the ball is the single most important element in all strokes of tennis. Without a good understanding of it, further progress in the game is difficult, if not impossible.

Control of the ball is best explained at the point of contact. This is where the racket face (strings of the racket) and the ball make contact with each other. It is important that the racket face be at the proper angle to direct the ball to its desired target. By adjusting the racket face angle you will be able to vary the direction of your hit i.e., a racket face tilting with its strings to the sky at contact will send the ball in that direction — to the sky or upward. A racket face angled to the right at contact will direct the ball to the right. It is this deflection of the ball off the face of the racket that directs where the ball will go. As logical as this may seem, it is one of the most misunderstood basics of the game.

Now that you realize the ball will travel in the direction your racket face dictates at contact, you will begin to have a better understanding of how to direct the ball. The essentials of a stroke — positioning, backswing, and follow-through — are only important in relation to ball control at contact. Players often try to adjust or correct their strokes by implementing new techniques they might have read about or heard mentioned, never really understanding how these changes relate to their overall stroke. Remember that *all* changes or adjustments to a stroke should be done so as to improve your control of the ball.

To increase your ability to control the ball it is important to understand how to "lengthen your contact." Once the racket face makes contact with the ball, the racket should continue moving through the ball in the direction of the desired target. This should give you a clearer understanding of the follow-through of a stroke. The term's real meaning is to follow *through* the ball, not to end somewhere out in front of the body or wrap around the neck as many might think. This long contact with the ball allows for more control, in that it offers a "guiding" effect the longer the ball is kept on the strings. The shorter the contact, the greater margin for error of control. This is the reason that players who use excessive wrist action on their strokes are known to play erratically. The racket face comes across the ball in a quick slap, rather than through the ball in a controlled drive. This shortened amount of time that the ball remains on the strings requires precision timing at contact for accuracy.

Big topspin players also usually play with a short contact on their stroke. Their racket travels from underneath the ball and finishes above it in a "brushing" movement up the back of the ball. It is important to understand that to get better control of these shots in tennis, the ball needs to remain on the strings longer.

The "seven-ball method" works well for visualizing what the racket head needs to do to accomplish a longer contact. Line up seven balls one behind the other in a straight line somewhere on the court. Position yourself behind this line of balls and simulate your stroke (either forehand or backhand) over the path of the seven balls. The first ball represents where the contact will take place. Stop your swing at the envisioned contact the first few times to check that your racket face is in the desired angle to direct the ball. It should be in the same straight line that the seven balls represent. Then continue your swing keeping the racket face at the same angle to guide the ball to your target. Count all seven balls as you simulate following through them. You've just demonstrated a long contact with your stroke. As you play, use this seven-ball method to imagine that you are hitting seven balls instead of one. Your contacts will be longer and you'll find that you have a better "feeling" for the ball as it remains on the strings of your racket longer. You will also discover that you'll be able to direct the ball with much better control over it.

Whether you are playing a baseline game, serving and volleying, playing offensively or defensively, ball placement is the key in tennis. This applies to one- and two-handed strokes, left or right handers, men, women, and junior players. Power without placement is like speed without control. Everything is geared to ball control in tennis — footwork, positioning, balance, rhythm, grips, spins, strokes, and strategy. You cannot control your play until you have learned to control the ball.

Have a target for every shot that you hit in tennis. If the ball doesn't go to your target there will be a reason why it didn't. Understanding this reason will help you learn how to get better control over your shots. Strive to improve your control over the ball and watch your level of play elevate.

⚹ ERRORS ARE HOW YOU WIN POINTS

There are only four mistakes you can make with the ball: hit it into the net, over the baseline, too far to the right, or too far to the left. This is a way to help you keep errors "simple" so that you can better understand them. The name of the game then becomes avoiding errors and playing consistent tennis. Even though this may be the most basic of the basics, it is forgotten time and time again. Your ultimate tactic in tennis should be consistency, no matter at what level you play the game.

The typical tennis match is two players trying to *give* each other each game by making a series of errors until finally someone gives the match away. The winner feels like he has won the match because he was the better player, and the loser feels like he has lost because he has beaten himself. Actually the loser just gave away the match first! Most matches are *lost*, not won. Remember that usually the player with the fewest errors will be the winner.

Few players realize that most points in a tennis match are over after three to four hits. If they could just learn to keep the ball in play, they would greatly increase their success with the game. Even at the professional level, approximately seventy percent of all points are won due to errors. It follows that as the level of expertise of the players decreases, the percentage of points won from errors will increase accordingly.

Don't let the net be your biggest obstacle. This is where the majority of errors are made in tennis. The next time you play, think that you must hit over "two nets" instead of one to give yourself a higher margin for error. "Lift" the ball on your stroke, swinging from low to high to get the ball to clear the net with a greater margin.

Errors are also common when players simply aim too close to the side or baseline. A tip to remember is "Aim a yard from the line and you'll be just fine." Tennis is said to be a game of inches and players often use every inch of the court with their shots. Allow yourself a comfortable margin for error on all your strokes and avoid unnecessary errors that occur when you aim too close to the net or lines.

Another instance when you are likely to make an error is when you are out of position. This is not the time to try a spectacular winning shot with a low chance for success. A lob would offer a higher margin for error and would give your opponent a chance to make the error first. Give him that opportunity to make the error first, don't try to beat him to it!

Learning to play percentage tennis will certainly help reduce the number of errors you make in a match. That is, play the shots which allow you maximum effectiveness but with a high margin for error. It is a common misconception that the pros hit very low to the net and aim for the lines on most strokes. The consistently winning pros understand percentage tennis and keep most balls three to six feet above the net and several feet from the side and baseline. They will place the ball close to the net and the lines only if the match situation calls for these lower percentage shots. They play aggressively when necessary, however, they don't gamble unreasonably.

Errors can be either *forced* or *unforced* in a match. Your opponent can force you to make an error by playing a shot that is too difficult for you to handle. An unforced error is usually a routine shot that was missed because it was carelessly played. The number of both forced and unforced errors that you make can be greatly reduced by your understanding what causes the error to happen.

Cross-court shots are good shots to play to avoid making errors. The net is six inches lower in the center of the court and there are approximately six and one-half more feet of court to hit into on the cross-court angle, as compared to the straight down-the-line shot (78' versus 84½').

The next time you're out practicing, try hitting five strokes before you attempt to win the point. This will help you learn to keep the ball in play longer. You'll also discover how much more in control of your strokes you will be as you get into a better rhythm from the longer rallies you've created.

Understand that errors are how you win points in tennis. Learn to play consistently and give your opponent a chance to make the error first. Play the game with a higher margin of error on your strokes to produce consistent results. You can win most matches by simply remembering the most basic of all basics — keep the ball in play and avoid making errors.

♀ LINE UP YOUR BODY PROPERLY

Footwork is necessary to place your body in the proper position to hit the tennis ball. To consistently move your body into the correct position takes time and practice. At first, judging the bounce of the ball will be difficult, but through practice it will become much easier to anticipate.

Let me first say that there is no one right way to hit a tennis ball. Look at all the different styles and strokes used by the top players in the game. Some like to turn sideways to the net while stroking (closed stance), others like to face the net (open stance). Some prefer to step into the shot with their right foot, while other like to use their left. Some like the balls high, others prefer them low. The most important thing is for you to discover what "contact zone" feels comfortable to you.

Your "contact zone" is the area in which you make ball contact in relation to your body and its distance away from the ball. This contact zone should be somewhere between your shoulders and knees and a comfortable distance away from your body without excessive reaching or cramping. Footwork will then be important to bring you into this position consistently. Your body in effect needs to be *lined up* to meet the ball properly. The closer you get to the contact zone, the more care you should take in your positioning. Shorten your steps and strive for an exact position of your body for the most comfortable hit possible.

The pros understand the importance of positioning and have learned to line up their bodies to make their strokes look easy. Their arms don't have to make all the awkward adjustment to make contact with the ball that most club players do. They have learned to use their feet instead. They use "fast feet and slow racket" on their strokes. That is, they move quickly but do not rush their strokes in the process.

Your body should remain behind the ball on all strokes. This will allow for more control as well as better angles for placement. It also will save you from the many possible injuries such as tennis back, shoulders, wrists, and elbows that result from taking the ball at your side or behind you. The most common injuries occur when a player repeatedly takes the ball late and uses the arm, wrist, or shoulder to *muscle* it over the net. When the body is not behind the ball on groundstrokes, the player must compensate by putting more pressure on the arm. A server who commonly hits serves at his side or behind him will likely experience back or shoulder pain as he overuses these body parts to compensate for lining up to the ball improperly.

Not only can your body position create bodily injuries, it can also affect your ability to play better tennis. Usually the more advanced the level, the earlier the ball is taken, that is, out in front of the body. Advanced players realize that the earlier they take the ball the less time their opponent has to react to the shot. They might even take the ball "on the rise" or play the ball as it rises up from the bounce rather than waiting for it to reach its peak and hitting it as it descends like most players do. It is easier to play the ball by moving forward to it, but timing adjustments will be needed if you plan to stroke the ball "on the rise."

Your reaction time must be fast and your footwork quick to get into the proper position after your opponent hits the ball. Players often move too slowly after their opponent has hit the ball, sometimes not even reacting until the ball has cleared the net. They tend to rush over at the last moment to contact the ball and hurry through most shots, producing hectic play and poor control. Learn to be quicker off your opponent's hit and see how relaxed and smooth your strokes will become. Step towards the ball to take it earlier, and keep it in front of your body. Your positioning will help you direct and control your shots if you learn to line your body up properly.

⚡ ADJUST YOUR PREPARATION

Preparation is everything that leads up to the point of contact in a stroke. Adjustment implies flexibility and versatility. This includes how ready you are to get your body and racket in position to make the proper contact with the ball. Preparation begins with the "ready position." The intensity that you demonstrate in this position should be set according to the situation and the stroke. If you are hitting casually from the baseline with another person on the opposite side of the baseline, your intensity wouldn't be the same as if you were at the net against someone hitting hard passing shots by you. Often players simply get into the ready position for all strokes and situations with the same level of intensity. Learn to adjust your intensity as the situation demands and according to the time that you have to prepare.

Grips prepare the racket face for the proper angle to hit the desired shot. John McEnroe, Jimmy Connors, and Bjorn Borg all use different grips to accomplish a similar task. Although their grips vary, they are all correct. There is a lot of argument over which grip is best and offers the fewest limitations, however, the fact remains that throughout history there have been a variety of grips used by great players. Experiment to find the grip that feels most comfortable to you and that allows you the most control over your shots. Be able to adjust to get the desired grip in the time prior to contact with the ball.

It is important to realize that all of the great tennis players prepare for their shots on the approach, while other players prepare for their strokes once they reach the ball. This early preparation allows for a smooth and controlled stroke with plenty of time allowed. Rushed and hurried strokes are usually a result of late preparation of body and racket.

It is not always necessary to have a backswing to properly

prepare your racket to make contact with the ball. A volley, for example, or a hard hit ball right at you, usually won't allow you the time to take your racket back. Touch shots also don't require the power you gain by taking your racket back. Your backswing, therefore, should be adjusted according to the shot played to you and the shot you wish to play.

The height of the bouncing ball you are about to strike will also require an adjustment if you are not hitting it at the same height each time. Your backswing should be adjusted up or down according to the height of the ball. High bouncing balls remain one of the most difficult shots for most players to play. This is because they haven't learned how to adjust their backswings accordingly. They keep their racket height the same for all shots regardless of the height of the ball. It's important to learn how to adjust your racket preparation to be in control of balls hit at all heights.

Backswings for groundstrokes usually come in two forms — "straight back" and circular or "loop" swings. The "straight back" method is an efficient one that wastes little time or effort. The "loop" backswing is favored by the majority of professionals. They like the better rhythm and timing they receive on their hits by keeping the racket moving throughout the entire stroke. There will be times when a "straight back" is needed for harder or quick reaction shots. A "loop" swing might be best at times for low balls to help you get under the ball to lift it over the net. It is important to understand both backswings and to be able to adjust for each.

As a rule of thumb, a full backswing at the baseline, a half backswing at the service line, and no backswing at the net. The closer you come to the net, the shorter your backswing should be because less power is needed to get the ball over the net. Your reaction time must also be quicker the closer your opponent is to you. Learn to adjust your preparation to allow for good control of the ball. If you are uncomfortable and feel rushed with your strokes, smooth them out by preparing yourself earlier to make the contact you desire. Your flexibility in preparing to meet the ball will determine your ability to keep good control over the ball in a variety of situations.

♀ POWER, SPIN, AND DEPTH — QUALITY OF BALL CONTROL

Everyone likes to hit the ball hard, right? But who likes uncontrolled power? No one! Power should not be used at the expense of control, but rather it should be used to form a higher quality of control.

How can you achieve more power in your game and yet still retain the necessary ball control? Contrary to popular belief, swinging harder at the ball will not necessarily hit the ball with more speed. Power lies in the technique and timing used to get your racket into the proper position to make contact with the ball. Usually a smooth and graceful but well-timed hit will generate more ball speed than a wild swinging one. The reason for this is solid contact with good racket control. It has been said that players who hit with good length on their contact hit a "heavy ball." The ball travels at a higher speed simply by allowing more force from the swing to go through the ball in sending it back over the net.

Advanced players understand how to use their opponent's pace to send the ball back faster. With proper timing, they drive through the ball with less effort and create more power for themselves in the process. A firm wrist is of utmost importance for controlling powerful volleys and groundstrokes. "Wristy" players can usually whip a lot of power into their strokes but rarely with sufficient control.

To achieve more power with your groundstrokes, make sure that you can generate enough force from your backswing to send the ball at the desired speed. A shortened backswing will generally not have enough forward momentum to hit a powerful shot unless your stroke is well timed and you use your opponent's pace.

Beginners use gravity to keep the ball in play, while advanced players use spin. This ability to spin the ball with control is often what separates the levels of players.

Spin is created on the ball as the racket, at impact, "brushes" the backside of the ball, either upward for topspin or downward for backspin. The amount of spin will vary according to the length of contact and force of the swing. The shorter the length of contact the more spin will be generated because more "brush" will take place on the ball.

Exact timing then becomes necessary to control a ball with lots of spin because it remains on the strings for such a short time. The pros understand this, and that is why they can hit with such tremendous amounts of spin and still retain total control of the ball. They stroke the ball using spin to increase the quality of control they have over it. Club players on the other hand sometimes struggle with controlling balls hit with lots of spin. They emulate the pro's swings but never understand how to tame the wild spinning ball that they have created.

The players who play this game for a living have not only hit literally millions of balls, but they practice daily to keep their games sharp. They understand the exact timing necessary to hit the ball with such a short contact and still retain control of it. Hopefully, you now understand that to consistently hit spin with control, your contact must be lengthened (in other words, you must hit through the ball) and without an extreme brush across the back of the ball. If you still insist on hitting with big spin like the pros, work to develop better timing through repetitive practice.

A spinning ball will behave differently than one hit without spin. A ball hit with topspin will drop sooner than it would with the force of normal gravity on it. This is why topspin has become so popular over the years with big hitters who like power but lack the necessary control to keep the ball in the court. An upward-moving racket will generate topspin on the ball. A topspinning ball rotates forward and downward which helps bring the ball down into the court after it has cleared the net.

Conversely, a ball hit with underspin tends to stay in flight longer. The shot is sometimes called a "floater" as the ball can hang up in the air almost as though floating or sailing. A ball that is struck from a downward-moving racket will create an underspinning ball. A "sliced" or underspinning ball will spin in the opposite rotation from the topspin. It is the backspin of the ball that creates a drag in the airflow underneath, keeping it afloat. A ball is hit with underspin to keep the ball down once it bounces. When an underspinning ball hits the court, it has a tendency to stay low and not bounce up nearly as high as a regular bouncing ball would.

You can achieve "depth" with your hits by keeping the

ball deeper in your opponent's court. This advanced form of placement can dramatically increase your level of play by making your shots much tougher for your opponent to handle. A ball that is hit shorter or mid-court to your opponent is handled with relative ease. However, a ball that is played within several feet of the baseline is a much more difficult shot for your opponent to play. Your opponent will have a shorter time to react and must adjust his swing and balance to handle your deep shots. The usual result is that he is forced to make a poor return.

To find the right depth, adjust the net clearance trajectory of your shots. Allow a good margin for error by not aiming directly at the baseline. Think of power, spin, and depth and the quality of ball control. As you wish to advance your game, work to increase your control of the ball by developing a higher *quality* of control over it.

℞ THE GAME'S MOST IMPORTANT STROKE

If you had your choice of having just one invincible stroke in tennis, it would be your serve. Half of all points that you'll play in a match will begin with your serve. It is the single most important stroke in tennis because no one stroke can offer you as much success as the serve can.

The serve is a complex stroke that requires a unity of body movements to execute properly. "Never before have I been required to perform so many tasks at once," say the beginners. To better understand the serve, let's simplify it. A serve is performed similarly to other strokes in that it is important to have a good "contact zone" for controlling the ball. The advantage of the serve is that you alone control the stroke. The variable of playing a moving ball hit to you by your opponent is eliminated. The service toss then becomes important to place the ball into the desired "contact zone," which should be a comfortable distance away to allow for an outstretched arm at contact.

Let's take a look at how to control a serve. Unless you're over eight feet tall, you'll need to hit *up* on the ball to get it to clear the net. This is probably the single most misunderstood aspect of the stroke. Time and time again the serve will land in the net leaving the server perplexed as to what happened. A netted serve occurs when the server simply hits *down* on the ball. Just as in all strokes in tennis, the ball will travel left, right, straight, up, or down according to the angle of the racket face at contact.

A tip to help you better understand how to direct a serve: think of the ball as a clock. Swing up and forward to hit the right side of the ball, or three o'clock, to send the ball to the left. Swing up and forward to make contact with the ball where the clock's hands meet, or in the center of the ball, to hit a straight ball. Swing up and forward to hit the ball at nine o'clock to send it to the right. In each of these examples, the racket face angle at contact was facing its desired target.

To improve your serve, strive for quality of ball control. The ability to place the ball deep in your opponent's service box will greatly increase your success with the stroke. It will produce a more difficult shot to return. Adjust your "hitting up" on the ball to find the right net clearance and allow for good depth on your serve.

Spins are achieved as they are with groundstrokes by shortening the contact of the racket face by brushing the ball instead of hitting *through* it. Contact with a brushed racket face across the ball at three o'clock produces a slice or side spin on the ball. A ball brushed up the back at six o'clock produces topspin. The amount of spin will vary with the amount of contact and force behind the swing.

You can increase the speed of your serve by learning to accelerate your racket head through the ball. Increasing the speed of the ball does not necessarily require a harder swing. Proper timing and contact are essential to a more powerful serve. Hold your racket with a relaxed wrist on the serve. As you go through the service motion, the racket will extend from behind the head to meet the ball overhead with a full, outstretched arm. It's at this point that the relaxed wrist allows the racket head to accelerate up and through the ball for increased speed. Beginners and many intermediates often keep a firm wrist throughout the serve. They could in all likelihood hit a much harder ball if they would just let their *racket do more of the work,* instead of forcing their arm to do it all. Keep the ball at a comfortable distance in front of your body to allow your body's force to get behind the stroke. A ball tossed to your right or straight over your head will likely only get the force behind it that your arm,

Notice the ease of Ken Rosewall's stroke. His racket has effectively travelled through the ball and finishes pointing directly to his intended target.

The fluid movement of Ken Rosewall as he glides about the court. His balance remains perfect while his eyes stay fixed on the ball. (As seen during the Grand Masters Tennis Tournament at Bluewater Bay.)

back, or shoulder can generate. This will not only limit your power, but can also place undue stress on those body parts that must compensate for lack of proper use. This is often how tennis injuries occur.

As important as the serve is in tennis, it amazes me how little emphasis most players place on this stroke. Few spend the necessary time to practice it, try to direct it, try to vary the speed and spins on the balls they hit with it, or even try to win it. If you could do nothing but hold (win) your serve in every tennis match, you couldn't be beaten! The worst that could happen is that your opponent would extend you into a tie-breaker each set. If you could hold your serve throughout the tie-breaker, you couldn't lose that either. What a strategy! Develop a winning serve and you can't be beaten!

Take your time on your serve. Don't be so anxious to rush into the stroke. This is one stroke that you have complete control over because you decide when you're ready to begin the point with it. Just as with all strokes in tennis, the majority of service errors occur when you *rush* the stroke. Relax and let your stroke flow smoothly. Bouncing the ball several times and taking a deep breath before you serve each ball could be the trick that brings your serve back to life.

Learn to control and place the ball on your serve. Every shot should have a target in tennis, including the serve. Vary your placement and work to confidently control its direction. Develop your serve into an important part of your game by increasing the quality of your ball control through increased speed, spins, and depth. Let your serve help you to become the best player that you can be. Learn to hold your serve and you'll discover that it will become much easier to win matches.

⚲ MORE SUCCESS WITH LESS EFFORT

Ken Rosewall has always been a player who makes the game look easy. He looks so smooth and effortless in his play, and yet his accuracy is uncanny. His nickname is "Muscles," which he has been called over the years because it is such a contradiction to his style of play.

The majority of players haven't learned his secret of "matching the effort to the task." Nothing seems to be wasted with his style of play. He uses an economy of motion, or simply a controlled swing to hit a controlled ball.

Most players attempt to *muscle* the ball or *try* to hit it harder by straining and using brute strength to accomplish their task. They often punch or flick at the ball trying to speed it up. Some may even tighten all the muscles in their arm to try to bring added power to their stroke. It's not jerky, fast-moving rackets that hit the ball harder, rather it is slower, efficient, and effective swings that drive the force of the swing through the ball.

Shots in tennis are most often missed when strokes are rushed or hurried. Players then search for new strokes to correct the problem, when smoothing out and letting old strokes "flow" is really the answer. Don't *try* so hard when stroking the ball. Relax and learn to "match the effort to the task" on your strokes. Over-hitting with wasted power and energy is senseless. Slow your swing down and concentrate on a long contact. Let the force of your swing travel through the ball. The result will be an efficient and effective swing without any wasted effort.

Efficiency can be very important in long matches, on hot days, and as you get older. The need to save your strength can be the intelligent tactic that you've been searching for to play a better game of tennis. Hectic, jerky strokes that accelerate the racket unnecessarily waste precious energy and can tire you in a long match. A flowing, rhythmic stroke can drive the ball with a lot less effort and produce better results. You'll tire less quickly and will remain fit to play longer.

Your movement can also be made economical to help conserve energy. Flow with your stride and remain lower to the ground with low, gliding steps. Avoid wasting energy by picking your feet up too high.

You can become a more effective tennis player simply by learning to slow down your swing and let all the force of your racket go through the ball. Use a controlled swing to hit a controlled ball and you'll discover more success in tennis with less effort.

⚘ *BACK TO THE BASICS*

When you start having trouble with your game, learn

to do as the pros do — go back to the basics. This is why it's so important to have a good understanding of the basics and to be confident in your ability to execute them. Without this knowledge, you'll be stuck with your game with nowhere to turn. This often happens to players who reach a plateau with their games. They want to proceed further with their tennis, but haven't been able to properly develop their strokes because they've been built on faulty basics.

When trouble begins with your strokes, chances are it has to do with the way you are controlling the ball. Remember that everything in tennis (footwork, body positioning, racket preparation, etc.) is to prepare your racket to make proper contact with the ball. Are you directing the ball where you want it to go? If not, why? Search to understand the reason. To increase your control over the ball, lengthen the contact on your strokes. Don't be so anxious to have the ball come off the strings of your racket so fast. Keep it there a little longer until you "feel" the ball and your strokes come back to form.

Footwork and body positioning are other basics that you might need to focus on. Line your body up to control the ball better. The pros realize that grooved strokes don't just happen. They occur because proper body positioning has taken place. Get your feet moving!

Take a look at your errors. Are you attempting un-reasonable shots and taking unnecessary gambles? Get the safest margin back into your strokes with a "two net" net clearance and "a yard from the line" target. Don't beat yourself, concentrate on consistency to get your form back.

In order to believe in your basics, you must have strokes you can count on. This is why a limited number of strokes is often better to have than a huge arsenal. You've all heard of the "Jack of all trades who is master of none." Possessing a chip forehand, a drive forehand, a topspin forehand, a slice forehand, and a touch forehand does you no good if you can't rely on one of these forehands when it matters most in a match. Talented players are sometimes at a disadvantage here. Instead of having such a range of strokes, focus your talent on fewer strokes that are more accurate and consistent. You will become more confident of your basics in the process, and will have the ideal foundation on which to build your game.

⚮ SUMMARY

Tennis players often play the game out of sheer fascination for the sport. It is important to understand and develop a solid foundation in the basics, because this is what your game is built on. Ball control is the single most important element in all strokes in tennis. To increase your control over the ball, learn to lengthen your contact. Take aim at a target for every shot you hit in tennis. Stop giving points away; reduce your mistakes by playing with a higher margin for error on your strokes. Line your body up for a comfortable contact. Adjust your preparation to keep good control over the ball in a variety of situations. Strive to increase the quality of your control of the ball by applying power, spin, and placing the ball deep.

Develop your serve into an important part of your game. It can open many doors to your tennis future. Let the force of your swing travel through the ball. You will find that you're able to hit an effective stroke with an efficient swing. Develop your confidence in a limited number of strokes that you can count on. These are the basics on which you build a winning game.

CHAPTER 2

Realize
Your Potential Through
Self-Control

℺ *YOU ARE YOUR OWN TOUGHEST OPPONENT*

You've already learned how you can beat yourself by making errors and giving points away in a match. But there are several other ways that tennis players have been known to beat themselves. Let's take a look at some of these and see if you can learn how to prevent them happening to you.

Strange things happen sometimes at the tennis courts. Calm, well-liked, and subdued individuals can undergo a Dr. Jekyll/Mr. Hyde transformation right before your eyes when they get into competitive situations. These players simply lose control of themselves. It might be over a bad line call or a reaction to a mistake or some other ill-timed condition that sets them off. It is usually easy for these same people to keep their composure when everything is going their way and a smooth match is being played. However, let something interfere or change the flow of a match and watch out!

To retain control of yourself through all situations, good and bad, takes a great deal of mental strength. Complete control over your emotions in a tennis match is not easy to accomplish. However, if you want to perform consistently to your ability, self-control is a vital requirement. Without control, your mind is never allowed to focus for any length of time, hindering your performance. You become too concerned with the many distractions and dwell on them until the situation controls you, instead of you controlling the situation.

A temper is never a pretty sight. No one ever gains in a tennis match by expressing anger or showing his temper. People seem to think, "Well, that's just me, I can't change it." Everyone has a temper, even the most mild-mannered people who never seem to get their feathers ruffled at anything. They have simply learned to overcome it and stay in control. A temper can be like a cancer; it can consume your body and adversely affect your play. All aspects of temperament, even in the most hot-headed of players, can be mastered to restore control in all situations.

When you're in control of yourself, losses and poor play won't bother you as much. That's not to say that you'll lose your competitive edge or "killer instinct." It just means that you won't have to outwardly express your anger and aggression on the court. You'll discover that you'll automatically exhibit better sportsmanship and court behavior, not to mention consistent play with better results. By keeping your composure you'll show a little more integrity and class, and you'll start to feel more like a professional.

Be at ease with yourself. Don't let the distractions control you. They are probably affecting your opponent as much as they are affecting you, so let them affect him while you remain in control. Eliminate the negative self-talk. You can convince yourself of anything if you repeat it enough, so why try to bring on your temper? Don't let yourself become your own toughest opponent.

A MASTER OR A VICTIM OF YOUR ATTITUDE

You and you alone are responsible for your attitude. You accept that responsibility by being the person that you allow your attitude to make you. You are your attitude because your attitude controls who you are. It shapes your actions and your responses.

People are just about as happy as they make up their minds to be. Your entire mood and outlook on life is dictated by your attitude towards it. You can choose to let it bring you down or you can let it raise you to great heights. The choice is yours, you're in control! People who are often seen in good spirits are not that way by accident. They are in the right frame of mind because they have chosen to be.

How does this affect you as a tennis player? Probably the worst problem you'll ever face in tennis is a bad attitude. Time and time again I've seen this destroy a good player. It blocks out a person's willingness to learn, causes mood swings, and slowly breaks down their self control. It is sad to see this happen. Tremendous tennis abilities can be wasted when a bad attitude sets in.

Attitudes can be shaped and molded over the course of time. You see, attitudes are nothing more than habits of thought. Being aware of your attitudes and how they affect you is the first step in controlling them. With willingness, desire, and discipline of your thinking, you can make your attitude into whatever you want it to be.

Learn to think positive thoughts and block out those that are negative and self-defeating. When you stop having fun, you'll probably stop winning. So enjoy yourself and think on happy thoughts. Another way to train your mind for a healthy attitude is to put your life into perspective. If you're unhappy for a reason, think of all the things in your life you have to be happy about. Write them down and look at them as often as you need to put yourself into a better or more desirable mood. If you remind yourself of the many problems in your life or of the many mistakes you've made in your match, you will suffer all the more from it. Remember the good shots that you've hit and dwell on those to pick yourself back up. If that doesn't seem to work, put the match into an even larger perspective. Think of how really insignificant your problems are in comparison to the many problems in world, such as hunger, war, and corruption. How lucky you are to have only to deal with such problems as missing a silly forehand into the net!

Be enthused about playing tennis today and feel great about it! You'll be amazed at how this attitude change can affect your play so positively. Practice it often to ingrain good habits of thought. You'll discover that anything will become possible in tennis when you learn to play it with the right attitude.

ADJUST YOUR INTENSITY LEVEL

Everyone has an optimum intensity level at which he

or she performs best. To find the level of intensity which will bring about your best performance, you need to learn to adjust your intensity and find what works best for you. Arousal levels, as they are called by psychologists, are levels of intensity that can be controlled through practice. You can learn to *psych yourself up* as well as *psych yourself down* according to the level of intensity you desire.

Most players tend to become overexcited and aroused when playing tennis. They rush their strokes and are generally too uptight or intense to play their best. They would probably find that they could play a much higher level of tennis by simply toning down their intensity, or learning to psych themselves down. To slow down your intensity while playing, simply slow down your breathing as well as the pace of your walk. Stop to tie your shoelace to gain a few extra moments to relax and adjust your intensity to a more desirable level. Even though giving 100% of yourself is ideal, trying too hard can ruin your efforts. Be intense with your play, but at a controlled level that you feel comfortable with.

Some players, such as John McEnroe, feel under-aroused and need to "pump themselves up" to reach their optimum level of intensity. They might feel that they are lacking energy or are unable to concentrate that day. Another sign of an under-aroused player is laziness or boredom. If you find that you need to psych yourself up while you're playing, increase your breathing, jump around to get the blood flowing, stretch or loosen up, and get your mind cleared to think in a more focused manner. McEnroe often excites himself through anger and outrage to pick up his intensity level. This isn't advisable for most people because very few players have been able to make anger work for them positively. It is usually an automatic self-defeater.

Pep talks can often bring about short-term positive responses, but to have any lasting intensity level changes, it is important to control your levels of anxiety, tension, and other emotional states. Experiment by noticing at which level you perform best. If you are currently playing at a level that hinders your performance, adjust your intensity by psyching yourself up or down accordingly. You can play at your ideal performance level every time by learning to control your intensity.

ℚ *AWARENESS OF WHAT YOU ARE DOING*

Have you ever watched someone who is out of control? They are completely unaware of what they are doing. Uncontrolled tennis players also lack an awareness of what they are doing.

When everything seems to be going wrong in a match it is time to stop and analyze exactly what is causing you to play the way you are. It might be the eighth double fault that you just hit into the net, or that all of your strokes are spraying over the baseline, or that your opponent appears to be cheating, and it has made you lose your concentration. When you're lost as to how to get your game back on track, remember this quote from Stanley Arnold, "Every problem contains within itself the seeds of its own solution."

To understand why you are playing the way you are, specifically address the problem. This is where the answer lies, and without directly analyzing it, you'll surely never understand how to correct it. To analyze the problem of a particular shot, ask yourself several questions. Is the ball going where I want it to? Why not? How can I correct it?

Take a look at your control of the ball. Is your contact long enough to give you good feeling on your shots? If your strokes are hurried, have you adjusted your preparation to adequately handle your opponent's pace? It is important not to make the same mistake over and over without some form of analysis and correction. At the professional level, players will rarely make the same mistake twice. They immediately analyze their errors and adjust accordingly. This is a keen awareness that you can develop through practice.

Being aware of your actions will help you learn to know what you're doing at all times on the tennis court. It will help prevent you from going into a daze and hitting seven forehands over the baseline without realizing it. Playing without an awareness of what you are doing will only bring about confusion, anger, and defeat. Instead, if you realize what is taking place after one or two have sailed long, you'll immediately ask yourself, "Why is the ball going long?" You'll analyze and correct it before you let it happen again. Learn from your mistakes, don't get angry with them. Let them help you become a better player with a sharper awareness.

You'll find that players who spend most of their time

judging their errors never learn to grow from them. They're too busy complaining about how badly they are playing to analyze and correct their problems. You'd think they would learn sooner or later, but they seem too involved in judging their shots to care about improvement. Don't let this happen to you. Be a controlled tennis player who is aware of what is taking place on the court. You'll be preparing to play the intelligent game of tennis that you aspire to.

⚲ LEARN TO SMILE AT MISTAKES

Everyone who plays tennis makes mistakes. But the players who know how to handle their mistakes and learn from them will be the great players in the future of this game. It's easy to wrinkle your face in anger when you miss a shot. It's a natural response of dissatisfaction. You want the whole world to see that kind of mistake is just not becoming to you.

Actually by making an outward expression of your unhappiness, you do several things. It will make you feel unhappy, which through repetition can develop into a bad attitude, and it can be a big psychological uplift for your opponent as he sees that you are disgusted with yourself.

Some of the greatest players in the game have learned to cool their responses to mistakes. Bjorn Borg, Ivan Lendl, and Chris Evert are all known for their "icy, emotionless" play. They appear so confident — as if they are unconcerned or indifferent that they've made a mistake. They have a look of assurance when behind, and rarely will they let an opponent see them frustrated.

This is the most difficult type of person to play against. You never feel like you're in the driver's seat, even when you might be. On the other hand, someone who is continually angry at himself after each mistake slowly digs his own grave. His opponent gleams with confidence at every outburst.

A smile is a mystical body expression. Have you ever tried smiling and not felt good afterward? Try it. Smile right now and notice how your face and body beam with joy. It's almost automatic. Your mind tells your body, "Feel good now" and you do. It quiets the nerves and brings about a state of calmness. The next time you're playing a match and you begin to get irritated at some of the mistakes you're making, try smiling at them. This will serve the purpose of telling the world, "Hey, can you believe I made a mistake?!" It will also keep your opponent guessing as to his control of the match because you will still appear to be confident and in control of yourself.

Grin if you miss your backhand wide. Your opponent might think that you're smiling because you realize why you missed it and you've learned from it. Maybe he thinks you're smiling because you're in control of yourself, or maybe he thinks you're smiling because you're in control of the match. You might simply be smiling to make yourself feel good, but you've sure got your opponent on the other side of the net worried about it! Actually your opponent is probably right. If you can exhibit that much self-control by facing your problems with such command, you've probably learned to be a mentally tough competitor. I'll put my money on you to win!

♀ *NO EXCUSE TENNIS*

Before you will ever be able to play tennis with complete self-control, you must learn to accept responsibility for your own actions. Your attitude and court behavior are no one and nothing's fault but your own. This is sometimes the most difficult concept to grasp. Clearly it is much easier to lay the blame on someone else or something else than it is to face the facts.

Have you ever known an irresponsible person to achieve much in life? Players who continually offer excuses are just that, irresponsible. They protect their egos with 1,001 excuses that they keep stored away for their protection. The worst part is that most of the time they really do convince themselves that this is the true reason for their failures. They will rarely search to understand the real reason for their defeat because they refuse to accept responsibility for it. They feel more comfortable blaming something else, but unfortunately they won't learn and grow until they face up to the real reasons for their defeat.

No excuse tennis means that you and only you are to blame for winning or losing. Every time you walk on the tennis court, you accept the responsibility of the challenge. Be open and honest with yourself. Don't resort to excuses and other such trickery. If you're feeling tired, don't start slumping your shoulders and dragging your feet. You can control your level of arousal. Pick yourself up, block out the tired feelings, and refuse to let yourself dwell on such defeating thoughts.

Preparation can play a vital role in eliminating most excuses. If you are ready to handle all opponents and conditions, certainly they won't affect you as much. Remember *not to let situations control you* by using the excuse of how they affected your play. Instead, *control the situation* so it is never allowed to affect your play adversely. To realize your potential in tennis, strive to play without excuses. You'll continue to learn and grow as a player if you'll accept the responsibility for your own actions.

⚲ SELF-DISCIPLINE

Discipline separates winners from losers, doers from talkers, and performers from those who simply have the potential to be performers. It is the necessary training that develops self-control in a person. A disciplined diet consists strictly of certain foods. A disciplined thinker will focus only on certain thoughts. A disciplined person adheres closely to a set of rules or guidelines. A self-disciplined person is totally in control of himself. He manages his own conduct and commands with authority his every action. He is at ease with himself because he has learned to master self-control.

Self discipline requires constant and well-regulated control. If you happen to lose your grasp of this control, it is because you aren't disciplined enough with yourself. People who have a difficult time breaking bad habits such as smoking, drinking, gambling, overeating, etc., lack the necessary self discipline. It takes patience, will power and persistence, but all of these bad habits can be changed into desirable ones. Your bad habits in tennis are just the same.

Learn to be strict and firm with yourself to conform to the standards you desire. How self-disciplined you are will determine just how good a tennis player you can become. To achieve total self control will take practice and training but most important, discipline of yourself.

♀ *PERMANENT POTENTIAL*

Some tennis players just seem to be stuck with their games in neutral. Their improvement has leveled off and they're on a plateau. These frustrated players appear to be in a state of "permanent potential."

Tennis coaches love to use the ambiguous term, "potential," to describe their students. It seems to be a welcome word to the ear of all who hear it used to describe them. But potential says nothing of fact. It is merely a word to describe something that has not yet occurred. Everyone has tremendous potential to achieve great things in life, but how many actually will?

Someone with "permanent potential" is playing the game with a misunderstanding. It might be a lack of knowing how to control the ball, or it might be that the player doesn't realize how to keep himself in control. If you find yourself reaching this state, progress out of it by searching for the necessary understanding. It is there to be found, but it will be up to you to find it and get yourself on the road to improvement.

Simply playing at this game offers few rewards. However, when you have an understanding of the game and of yourself, there is a limitless amount of enjoyment you can attain from the sport. Look to know and understand the game. Learn about yourself and how to gain discipline and self control in the process. Get a better understanding through an awareness of your play. Turn your mind "on" and play an intelligent game of tennis!

♀ *SUMMARY*

Don't let yourself become your own toughest opponent. Learn to control all situations and not let them control you. The worst problem you'll ever face in tennis is a bad attitude. You're responsible for your own attitude, so take control of it and shape it as you choose. Play at your optimum performance level by adjusting your intensity. Develop an awareness of what you are doing at all times to remain in control. Smile the next time you miss a shot, and see how it will help you remain calm. Be a responsible player and learn to play no excuse tennis. Discipline yourself to be a self-controlled tennis player. Reach your potential best by searching for a better understanding of yourself and of the game.

CHAPTER 3

Controlling the Focus of Your Mind

ℚ CONCENTRATION — THE HERE AND NOW

One of the most common phrases used by tennis players is "watch the ball." This is often said by players who are not trying to visualize the ball better, but rather are trying to focus their minds for better concentration.

Controlling your eyes while you're playing tennis can help you control your mind. Restricting your vision only to what is happening on the court and not allowing your eyes to wander outside the court can benefit your concentration. It will help keep you focused on what you should be concerned with. Allowing your eyes total freedom can often present too many distractions for the mind. If your focus is too broad, less attention is then paid to the task at hand. The more your mind is focused, the more intense your concentration and mental strength will be. For optimum performance, strive for a narrow focus of concentration.

Great unexplained feats have occurred when persons have channeled all of their thoughts and energy into a single task. This happens repeatedly in emergency situations where someone is in great need of help and a person lacking the necessary physical requirements is able to help them in a miraculous fashion. The fact is that there are very few things which can't be achieved once you set your mind to it. Some things might take longer than others, but with a focused mind and all your energy directed into a single task, the results can be achieved more efficiently and effectively.

47

Two people are watching the sun set together. One notices beauty in the vibrant colors of the sun as it sets against the soft blue sky. The other sees the sun, but his mind is too occupied with thoughts of the day and of his plans to notice its true beauty. His mind isn't focused on the here and now, so his concentration doesn't allow him to reap the enjoyment of the moment.

Blocking out past and future thoughts will help you to "moment compartmentalize" your thoughts. This will allow you to better concentrate on the present. Learn to focus only on the match, the ball, the point, the moment, the here and now. This is what concentration is. It is a skill that can be learned and developed through repeated practice. Concentration is really freedom from internal and external distractions. Most people will realize only about one percent of their mental potential, simply because they are unable to control their concentration.

In a tennis lesson, students will only be able to retain what they have learned as long as their attention is directed and focused on the subject matter. It is their attention span that will dictate how much they can learn during a given lesson. Very young players, such as those aged four to seven, usually have quite a limited attention span. The time period that these young players are able to concentrate is often only a few minutes. As they mature, their attention span gradually increases, allowing them more opportunities to learn. However, with this maturation also comes many distractions such as other interests, responsibilities, etc., which can greatly affect one's ability to concentrate.

As you continue to progress with your tennis game, the importance of controlling the focus of your mind will become apparent. Once you learn to focus your mind on the here and now, your attention and concentration can be controlled. There will be very few things you can't achieve in tennis once you set your mind to it.

⚲ DISCIPLINE YOUR THINKING

Donald Curtis summed it up best in the title of his book, *You Are What Your Thoughts Are.* You will always be a product of your thoughts. This is why disciplined thinking is one of the requirements for playing an intelligent game of tennis.

Self-talk is something all people do. Some like to talk out loud to themselves, while others prefer to keep their words only in their minds. How you talk to yourself will depend a great deal on what you are thinking. If you are thinking good and positive thoughts, you will probably be talking to yourself with words of encouragement. If you are thinking more negative thoughts, you will probably speak discouraging words to yourself.

Positive thoughts allow you to automatically relax as you feel more confident with yourself. Your concentration is then easier to hold because your mind is at ease. The problems of doubt in yourself and your tennis game begin when you lose control over your thoughts. You might be attempting a simple shot, but as soon as the thought of "I might miss it" enters your mind, you're in trouble. This is what is commonly referred to as the "power of suggestion." It can be your worst enemy or one of your dearest friends. It all depends on how you discipline your thinking.

If you've played tennis for any length of time, I'm sure you've seen how this "power of suggestion" can affect your play. Miss a first serve and just for a split second think that you might double fault, and sure enough, you will! This is a prime example of undisciplined thinking. Try suggesting to yourself instead that you will win the match and watch the determination and desire to win magnify within yourself. Your power of suggestion can affect you either positively or negatively, depending on what you're thinking.

Judging your play can negatively affect your concentration. Always be aware of what you are doing and understand how to correct your mistakes. However, refrain from criticizing yourself when you've made an error. This is the negative self-talk that you must learn to overcome. Strive to discipline your thoughts away from those of anger, worry, embarrassment, discouragement, guilt, frustration, confusion, depression, or panic. Learn to love the battle and train your thoughts toward success.

A wandering mind will focus nowhere, and too many thoughts will block out your ability to concentrate. Control your thinking so that it will allow you to be a relaxed and confident tennis player. To change your tennis game, begin by changing your thoughts. You will become the tennis player that your thoughts allow you to be.

BEING IN AUTOMATIC — "IN THE ZONE"

Players who have experienced playing tennis "in the zone" know what a truly wonderful feeling it is. Everything seems to work so well — almost automatically without any conscious thought. It is sometimes said that a player is playing "out of his mind" when this occurs.

When a player enters this state, he is only into his game. He isn't concerned with specific things that are happening on the court; they're just happening. He is totally aware, yet his actions are so automatic that little thought is required. This is a state of subconscious action with conscious decision making. The muscles are relaxed and the mind is attentive. The mind is completely focused on the present at a very high level and emotions are under total control.

It has been proven that an athlete's performance is hindered when analytical thought and self-judgmental talk occurs. Performance is at its peak when the athlete is more relaxed and playing more *instinctively*. Learning to trust yourself to be so relaxed and to let your mind take over will be difficult at first. However, the more you practice it, the greater your trust will become and the easier it will be to reach this state of "automatic pilot."

Your mind is the most complex computer in the world. If it has seen or hit a correct stroke in the past, it is capable of repeating it. Learn to relax and let your mind function to its ability. So often players never give their minds a chance to work up to their ability, as they cloud them with fears and anxieties. Your mind can remember every action that you've made depending on your level of intensity and attention span. You don't want to *try* to force the action to occur again. You want to visualize, relax, and do. Visualize the ball being directed along a path to your desired target. Breathe deeply, relax, and allow your mind to repeat this action in the stroke.

Try not to *think* about your strokes the next time you play. Relax and let your mind automatically make the shots. A common gamesmanship practice is to compliment someone on a particular stroke that they are hitting quite

Rod Laver is in perfect form and balance while instinctively playing this most difficult shot. (As seen during the Grand Masters Tennis Tournament at Bluewater Bay.)

well, only to see it fall apart once they begin to think about it. They had been hitting it naturally or automatically through their mind, and now they are thinking about it mechanically and have completely lost all feeling for the stroke.

Strive to get your body relaxed with your mind clear and focused. Learn to trust in your mind and its abilities, and let it take over and help you become a better player. You will continue playing the game aware of everything that is taking place, just performing more automatically. Discover how playing the game in automatic will bring about your best tennis performances. Let go and your mind will take you there.

♀ A GAME OF FEARS

Winners see what they want to happen while losers fear what might happen.

From the moment you take up playing the game through your progress in the sport to new levels, tennis will be a game of fears for you. You can overcome these fearful thoughts by learning to *think like a winner.* Visualize and think on positive thoughts that you would like to see happen. Avoid doubtful thinking on things that haven't even occurred yet.

Fears so often are created in the mind as players question how they appear to others. Beginners fear that they look like idiots, intermediates fear that they look like beginners, and advanced players fear they look like intermediates. It's a never-ending game of fears! Learn to block out how you think others might see you. Feel confident enough of your own abilities to be unconcerned with what others think. Remember that being nervous is only natural. All of the greatest players in the game have attested to their nervousness prior to and during their play. Control your nerves by not allowing fearful thoughts to enter your mind.

One of the best ways I've always found to overcome fear is to face it. If you can ask yourself the question, "What am I really worrying about?" you'll often discover that you won't even know what it is that you fear. The next question to ask yourself is "What can I do about it?" This will meet the fear head on and eliminate it, by bringing about rational thinking of proper action. Another way to deal with your fears is to face the worst possible outcome. You'll often find that the worst scenario isn't that bad after all. Your mind will then be much more relaxed and ready to face the situation in a more positive manner.

"Choking" is a term used in many sports to describe tentative play. Fear of making errors or of looking bad will cause you to choke. It will tense your muscles and hinder the smooth flow of your strokes. It also affects your ability to concentrate, as your emotional state is unbalanced. Realize simply that everyone is surrounded by influences that can affect them fearfully. Don't allow yourself to think like a loser, and fear what might happen. Be a winner and think what you want to happen!

✎ THE ART OF RELAXING

Do you realize how much tension you create in your body every day? What about right now while you're reading this book. Are you sitting in a relaxed position? Are the muscles in your arms and legs relaxed? What about the muscles in your shoulders and neck? Chances are, you're quite tense at this very moment. Learning to relax in your everyday life will help you relax much more easily every time you play tennis. The next time you're sitting in a chair or driving a car or walking the dog, practice relaxing yourself.

The most important thing to remember about relaxing is not forcing it. Don't *try* too hard to relax. This is never an effective way to relieve tension. Chances are that you'll only create more tension for yourself by thinking so hard about it. It must come effortlessly and easily or it won't come at all.

People who are in martial arts and Lamaze childbirth preparation classes realize the importance of breath control in relaxing the muscles. Breathing a slow breath sends a signal to the mind telling it that the body is relaxed and back in control. Advanced tennis players have discovered how exhaling on strokes can relax them and bring better ball control by lengthening their contact on the swing. They are often heard "grunting" as they strike the ball. This is so that their muscles won't tighten and cause a shortened stroke. By exhaling at contact, their muscles are more relaxed, so their strokes are longer and smoother.

Tension automatically increases as negative thoughts

enter the mind. Anxiety, worry, fear, and frustration can all tighten the muscles in your body and hinder your play. Positive thoughts, on the other hand, calm the mind and allow it to concentrate.

Self hypnosis and Transcendental Meditation are two ways through which you can reach a state of relaxation. Self hypnosis can be used to completely relax the muscles in your body. I became fascinated with this some years ago, and have used it with success to relax myself prior to playing important matches. Find a quiet place and focus your eyes on a tiny spot anywhere in your view. Start by mentally going to each body part and suggesting that it let go of all its tension and completely relax. Go to every part of your body including your tongue, eyes, etc., until your body is completely relaxed and free of tension. Continue to focus only on the fixed spot. Now slowly close your eyes to a count of ten. Once you've reached ten and your eyes are closed, you will be in a relaxed state with a free and clear mind. If you have reached this state just prior to playing a match, this is the ideal time to program your mind for a great performance on the court.

Transcendental Meditation uses the focus on a word called a "mantra" to block out all distractions. By repeating your chosen word over and over, your mind is made free of worry and tension. It is then at ease and can better focus itself.

Remember not to relax the mind, only the muscles in the body. A relaxed mind loses its focus, which can turn a match completely around. As soon as your mind thinks it has the match won, for example, it relaxes and thinks of what you have to do that afternoon or some other distracting thought, and suddenly your game starts to fall apart. Keep your mind sharp and in focus, but let your body be relaxed. You'll play a controlled game of tennis with smooth and relaxed strokes.

⚲ ANXIETY AND HOW IT AFFECTS YOU

Anxiety is one of the major causes of unintelligent tennis play. Feelings of anxiety can turn a smooth, relaxed stroke into a rushed, uncoordinated one. Corrective attention to a stroke is often prevented as anxiety obstructs concentration and impedes a focused mind.

Stress in itself is not bad as long as you can learn to manage and control it. When stress is not properly managed it can affect your body in a number of ways. The muscles tense when anxiety enters the mind, which can cause fatigue and injuries. If you have been tiring easily in your play, it might not be because of your physical limitations, but because your mind is not free and clear to allow a relaxed body. Injuries such as muscle cramps and pulls are also a direct result of muscle tension built up in the body from emotional anxiety.

Choking, which was discussed earlier, is what athletes call fear of failure. When a player chokes and misses a shot, his muscles are tense, his heart is racing, he has a clammy feeling, and he might even feel nauseated. This is all taking place because anxiety is present in his mind.

A tennis player experiencing feelings of anxiety during play will also be distracted, as concentration will be difficult to hold for any lengthy period. He might even discover a change in attitude as he loses confidence in his abilities because of his "off" day. He will, in all probability, develop more anxious feelings as he continues to play and might even stop trying because of his frustrations.

One way to free yourself from worry is simply to *relax*. *You cannot continue to worry if you are truly relaxed.* Stop judging yourself and your performance. Instead, try observing and correcting faulty strokes without passing judgment on them. This is what an intelligent tennis player does. Focus your mind, free from anxiety. Think positive, relaxed thoughts to produce positive, relaxed strokes.

℺ LET PRESSURE HELP YOU

So often players hit well in practice, but their strokes seem to fall apart in match play. What causes them to play so differently? *Pressure.*

Pressure is ever present in tennis. Competitive situations create pressure. Uncertainty also brings about a form of pressure. Being behind or even in a match can be a pressure situation. Playing big points, sustaining long rallies, and serving second serves can all apply pressure on you to produce as a player.

The easiest way to handle pressure is to remember that

pressure is something you put on yourself. *Winners respond to pressure while losers crumble under it.* Olympic track records are set in front of huge crowds when all the pressure is on. Some of the best tennis ever played has been in the finals of Grand Slam events when the intensity and stress were at their highest levels. The champions of the game have learned how to let a stressful situation boost their game, by directing the stress into energy, thus increasing their intensity.

To continue your quest to become the best tennis player you can possibly be, you need to let pressure help you get there. Learn to enjoy it and strive to get into as many pressure situations as you can. The greater the challenge, the greater your chance to reveal and discover your true potential. Learn to love the challenge and the battle of every pressure situation you play in.

I've always suggested, even to my beginning students, that they enter tournaments. It is here that you will discover what tennis is all about. You can easily find out what strokes need your attention, because they'll be the first ones to fold under pressure. You will also gain valuable experience necessary to developing into a confident tennis player. Be prepared to learn about pressure and how it can affect you. Practice as often as you can under pressure so that you will eventually be able to play even better under stressful circumstances.

Most players who have a difficult time handling pressure are the very ones who continually try to avoid it. They usually avoid playing in tennis leagues and tournaments and prefer instead to play socially. I'm not saying that this is an unacceptable way to enjoy the game. You'll probably reap much enjoyment form the fresh air and light exercise. However, if you want to realize your potential for the best tennis, pressure situations are necessary.

⚲ SUMMARY

Concentration is a freedom from internal and external distractions. Block out past and future thoughts to focus on the moment. Discipline your thinking to control the focus of your mind. Your mind is a complex computer. Once it is programmed, let it perform automatically for you. Winners see what they want to happen, while losers fear what might happen. Understand that tennis is a game of fears for everyone. Control your nerves by not allowing fearful thoughts to enter your mind. Relax the muscles in your body, but keep a sharp mind. If not properly managed, stress can make you play an unintelligent game of tennis. Think positive, relaxed thoughts. Pressure can ruin your play or bring you to your best performance. Learn to handle it and let it help you play your best tennis.

CHAPTER 4

You Can Win Even When You're Not the Best Player

LOOKS AREN'T EVERYTHING

Can you always tell who the best player is when you watch a tennis match? Will he always be the winner? Have you ever asked yourself *why*, when he didn't win?

When I first began playing tennis, the players who always impressed me the most were the flashy ones. The big hitters who could hit screaming winners an inch from the lines were the ones I liked. As I began to mature as a tournament player, I noticed how the consistent winners were often the most boring to watch. They didn't look impressive, so it was always difficult to rationalize how they could win.

One year while I was playing the National 21 and Under Circuit around the United States, I witnessed a match at Grossinger's Resort in New York which changed my view of the game. One of the top nationally-ranked players, who looked unimpressive to me, was playing against a player I thought should be a tough opponent for him. The top-seeded player, to my surprise, proceeded to take this guy apart. He hardly looked like he was moving, had no shots to hurt anyone with, and looked less than powerful, yet he took total command of the match and whipped his opponent in an effortless fashion. It had taken me quite a while, but I'd finally learned that looks aren't everything in tennis.

Since that time, I've seen many gifted athletes beaten by players with lesser physical abilities. Flashy players, I now realize, try too hard, are too intense, and have too much tension in their muscles to be relaxed and mentally in control. They might look impressive at times, but by carefully watching them perform over a period of time, you'll begin to see how little of their mental potential is ever used.

Some of the greatest tennis players ever have been less than imposing physical specimens. Rod Laver and Ken Rosewall are both under six feet in height and could be considered featherweights if they were boxers, yet between them they hold over twenty-eight Grand Slam titles! What has made these two guys such super athletes? They've learned to get the most out of their games by playing tennis intelligently.

Some elderly players who appear as though they couldn't beat anyone are often found to be quite good after they have you down 6-0, 3-0 in the match! They might lack the physical resources, but they make up for it by using their minds to play a clever game of tennis. Though they don't look like tough opponents, they often control the matches they play.

Have you ever watched a twelve-and-under junior girls' tournament? Some of these little girls can hit the cover off the ball! How can they hit harder, with more accurate strokes than most grown men? They have learned to hit efficient and effective strokes, putting better weight transfer and strength into their strokes. Their power isn't wasted in the swing. Instead, it is effectively directed into the contact and follow-through of the stroke.

Why is it so important to hit impressive shots? Strive instead to hit effective shots which produce more consistent results. Impressive players generally play with a small margin for error. They might play well one day, but will often play terribly the next. Remember that looks aren't everything in tennis. Play unimpressive shots that get the job done. You might be boring to watch, but you'll become a successful tennis player with consistent results.

DO YOU REALLY WANT TO WIN?

Asking yourself if you really want to win is not such a crazy question. So often matches are over before they ever begin. Many players have it in their minds that either they don't want to win, or they can't win. So the match is already lost in that person's mind. They usually go through the motions of playing out their defeat. You must decide before the match begins that you *want* to win if you ever expect to have the chance.

The most determined player on the court is the usual victor. They are the ones with the strong will and desire to win. Sometimes they have developed their tenacious attitudes out of necessity. It might be because they lack the other skills to be the better player on the court. They've learned to become mentally sharper instead and develop as fighters to make up for their shortcomings.

Maybe winning or losing isn't so important to you. Attempt instead to perform to the best of your ability — win or lose. Internally motivate and focus yourself on reaching your potential. This is the best attitude you could possibly have. You will then be comparing yourself only to you, and not to your opponent.

The next time you start winning and get a nervous, choking feeling, stop and think. You're probably not determined enough in your quest. Players who have a hard time putting matches away once they've built up substantial leads are usually lacking the necessary determination to complete the match. Refocus your mind and motivate yourself for a stronger will and desire for victory. *Someone who won't be beaten, can't be beaten.*

ℚ *SCORES CAN BE DECEIVING*

Some people have called the scoring system for the game of tennis the "craziest in any sport." "Fifteen," "thirty," and "forty" representing the winning of one, two, and three points is a little hard to accept at first. However, once you can get past the names for the different points, you'll find that the scoring system really presents a unique challenge.

In a single two out of three set match, the momentum or advantage of a particular player can swing back and forth between the competitors many times. After the score reaches even at *deuce* in each game, the winner of the game must win two points in succession. This can create a very good challenge for the competitors, as the game could last for an indefinite time. Games can often be decided with only a slight, two-point margin. Theoretically, a player could appear badly beaten with the scores being 6-0, 6-0, and still have played a very close match with his opponent in total number of points won.

It is even possible to win more points than your opponent and still lose the match. If, on the games that you win, your opponent scores no points (a love game), and the games that your opponent wins, you take him to deuce each time, it is highly possible to lose even when you have won more total points. Every game that you win would be by a margin of four points, and every game that went to your opponent would only have a two-point advantage. If you were to figure this out, you and your opponent could win the same total number of points, but you would lose the set 6-3 if your winning point margins each game are twice what his are.

It is also possible to win more games than your opponent and still lose the match. If the match goes to three sets and the set that you win is more in your favor than the other two sets that your opponent won, you can still lose after having won more total games. A score that reads 7-5, 0-6, 7-5 represents fourteen games won by the victor and sixteen games won by the loser!

Now it is easier to see how scores can be deceiving. It is not always the total number of points or games that decide the winner in a match, it is *where* and *when* the points and games are won that counts most.

There are many so-called "big points" that can be pivotal to the outcome of a match. Though all points count the same, there are definite advantages to playing them differently. The fourth point is considered by many players to be a big point in each game. If the score is 15-30 in your opponent's favor, it is important at this point not to let him get to 15-40, which will give him a higher percentage chance of winning. At 30-15 in your favor, the point also is a crucial one to get yourself to 40-15, which will give you the higher probability chance of winning the game.

The seventh game is considered the pivotal game in each set. When the score is 2-4 against you, it becomes a big game to get yourself back into the set. And at 4-2 in your favor, you don't want to allow your opponent back into the set by winning the game. At 3-3 it also becomes a critical game for gaining the momentum in the match and taking the lead.

Although these are recognized big points in any match, there are *many* times in a match when the point will be a big one or a game will be a crucial one. An example might be the first point in a match: it could be a big point to win if your opponent tends to lose control when he gets behind. Another big point to win could be your advantage in a game when your opponent is a determined fighter. It is a big one to win because he might be given the chance to come back if you don't end the game in your favor now. Another big point is when the match has been extremely close and the score is deuce. This is important to keep the momentum in your favor and the pressure on your opponent.

You'll find that the best players are the ones winning the key points and games in each match. It is not necessarily the total number of points and games you win that matters. Learn to recognize the big points and big games in every match that you play. Focus your energy and concentration to bring about your optimum play at these crucial times.

ℚ *YOUR OPPONENT PLAYS AS WELL AS YOU ALLOW HIM TO*

I'm sure you've all heard someone say that their backhand, volley, or entire game was "off" on a particular day. Although some players' games do fluctuate, what probably happened was that a clever opponent *made* him play poorly.

So many errors that are made in the course of a match are not due to your "off" day, but because your opponent is giving you shots that you don't like. Everyone has likes and dislikes, commonly referred to as strengths and weaknesses. You might be losing in a match simply because you're playing to your opponent's strengths and giving him the shots that are his favorites. This is when the old adage, "change a losing game," comes into play.

It's important to be able to analyze your opponent to discover his likes and dislikes. Try to be as specific as possible. Remember that the concern isn't just the forehand or backhand, but more specifically, does he like high or low balls, short or deep ones, hard or soft ones, close to his body or far away from him? How does he handle topspin, slice, and flat hit balls? Does he move well? Does he take big roundhouse swings at the ball? What is his pattern of play?

Once you start to see what kind of balls he likes to have hit to him, you can then make him "unhappy" by hitting balls that he dislikes. This isn't unsportsmanlike conduct, rather, it is the very essence of strategy and tactics in tennis. To play the kind of shots that your opponent dislikes might require you to play an entirely different game than what you're used to. World class professionals have to alter their games according to the opponents they face. This is one of the most difficult adjustments for the average club level player to make. They play every game exactly the same because they think, "That's the way I play."

Learn to alter and adjust your game to play to the dislikes of your opponent. If your opponent likes to charge the net, don't allow him to. Beat him to the net first, lob him, or keep the ball deep so that he won't have the opportunity to come in behind the short ball. If you watch closely, you can also see which stroke your opponent likes to come in on. Then simply don't allow him the chance to hit that shot; keep away from that particular stroke.

Your opponent might have a smooth baseline game with grooved strokes that make few errors. It looks like you've got a very tough opponent unless you play shots that change his pattern of play. Force him, rush him, pull him out of position, or play different spin shots that will throw off his rhythm and timing. Usually players who rely on grooved groundstrokes build their games on rhythm and timing. Anything you can do to break this pattern will force them to have an "off" day.

The great Bill Tilden, who was the World Champion for eight years between 1920 and 1930, used to play to his opponent's strengths. He said that if he could break them at their own game psychologically, they would be beaten with nothing to fall back on. For the advanced level player with a lot of confidence, there is no greater way to dominate an opponent. But, for the majority of players, the best way to beat your opponents is by exploiting their weaknesses. This doesn't necessarily mean you should play every shot exclusively to them. Mix up your shots and break your opponent's rhythm and pattern of play with a variety of shots that he doesn't like. Change the pace of your shots, the tempo of the match, and your style of play. Your opponent will never have had such an "off" day in his whole life.

ℚ READ YOUR OPPONENT

Have you ever noticed how some players seem to have an uncanny ability to be in the right place at the right time? Some players might say that it is luck or coincidence, while other call it good "court sense" or anticipation.

Anticipation can be learned and developed through the practice of reading your opponent. Your opponent has certain habits that are important for you to pick up on. Maybe he hits mostly cross-court on his forehand, he likes to serve to the backhand on second serves, makes most of his approach shots down the line, or returns all balls high over the net. To analyze his habits, try to see where he generally goes on a variety of different strokes. Anticipation is often no more than instant recall of a previous similar situation.

Your opponent can also tip you off on where he is going to hit the ball by how his body moves into the shot. Watch the way your opponent lines up to hit the ball cross-court and down the line. Does he line up the same way for these different shots? Watch the way his shoulders move into the shot. Usually you can tell where an opponent is going by watching his shoulders. If they begin moving early, look for an early contact or cross-court hit. If he waits until the ball is almost at his body before moving, look for a later hit or a down-the-line shot. Does your opponent step into the shot with his weight and keep the ball in front of his body? This will usually produce a solid, forceful shot. Or does he lean backward off-balanced to strike the ball at his side or behind him, taking the pace off the ball and generally sending it higher?

What your opponent does with his racket during the swing is another big clue as to what shot is about to be played. If your opponent winds up with a full backswing on a stroke, look for a powerful hit. If it is a shortened backswing, you might look for a softer shot to be played. The height of the backswing can also tip you off as to the type of spin about to be attempted. A higher backswing should tip you off that a slice or backspinning ball is coming. If it is a lower backswing, be on the lookout for the ball to be hit with topspin. The position of the racket face and follow-through at contact can also aid you in anticipating the next shot. If the racket face opens up with the strings facing the sky at contact, look for a higher shot, possibly a lob.

Learning to anticipate your opponent's shots requires an alert mind and a keen awareness. Read your opponent's strokes and his mind by understanding his habits, along with his body and racket motion. Good court sense is no more than a keen awareness of what your opponent is doing. Sharpen your mental skills by developing good practice in opponent analysis.

ℚ *KEEPING A PSYCHOLOGICAL ADVANTAGE*

Everything you are experiencing mentally in a tennis match is also felt by your opponent. It can create quite a struggle for you if you let it, or you can choose to let the struggle be your opponent's.

Rule number one is *slow down.* Don't rush around the court unless you are trying to speed up your slower-playing opponent. Take your time to make all of your actions *deliberate.* You won't have the psychological advantage over your opponent if you are rushed and in a state of panic.

Convince your opponent that he is going to lose by the respect you show him. This can still be accomplished in a cordial and friendly manner. Appear unimpressed when he hits a beautiful shot, and look unconcerned when you hit a silly error. Appear mentally tough and it will give you a distinct psychological advantage over your opponent. Self control and concentration are important. Your opponent should not get the edge because you appear rattled. Don't allow his confidence to grow by showing that you are fearful of him.

Play like a winner to keep the psychological advantage in a match. It amazes me how many players begin playing like losers when they get behind in a match. It's an automatic tip to your opponent that they're in control. A person who is losing often tries to hit winners to get back on top. A winner doesn't need to hit such low percentage shots. They have the lead, so they allow their opponents the opportunity to beat themselves by playing the low percentage shots. They don't have to try to hit winners to get back into a match, they're already ahead! To play like a winner, stop trying to make shots which have a one in ten chance of succeeding. Play steadily and allow your opponent the chance to lose his confidence and his lead by making the errors first.

Patience is definitely a virtue in the game of tennis. It alone can give you the mental edge needed to take control of a match. Someone who hits the ball with little or no pace can't hurt you unless you let it get to you mentally. Develop patience not to let their "bloopers" affect you. Be prepared to keep the ball in play one more stroke over the net than your opponent. Reverse it on them and see how they dislike it when you gain the mental edge over them with your patience!

Get control of yourself, your attitude, and your focus. Your opponent will see how concentrated and in control you are, and he'll feel threatened by it. Your mental edge will discourage him, as you'll appear to be an unfaltering player who can't be beaten.

✇ MAKE YOUR OPPONENT HIT THE BALLS YOU WANT

Your opponent can hit you all the balls you want in a match if you like. Isn't that nice of him? But first you must learn how to *make* him hit you those balls.

Notice the trend of your opponent's shots. Where does he like to play the ball most often? Observing these trends can help you set up a particular shot. You can play to the stroke that puts the ball there most often. For example, your opponent prefers to go cross-court on his forehand. He has been playing to your backhand repeatedly and you are wanting to use a forehand. Place the ball down the line from your backhand to his forehand and voilà — the long-awaited ball to your forehand is on its way.

Placing the ball to certain areas on the court can also limit your opponent's options for various shots. If you learn to recognize his limitations, you can get the balls you want from him by playing to these spots on the court. A well-placed ball hit close to the baseline will generally produce a short reply. If you are anxious to get to the net, this short ball will be the shot you want your opponent to hit to you. If your opponent has been wearing you down from the baseline, and you would prefer to hit your favorite lob or passing shot, hit a short ball which will automatically pull him into the position you desire and give you the chance to play your best shot.

Maybe you're normally a good volleyer, but your opponent has been getting the ball to your feet each time you approach the net. This has made it quite difficult for you to win any points at the net. Make him hit you the higher ball you've been longing for — keep the ball *low* to him as you approach the net. This will require him to hit the ball *up* to clear the net, giving you a chance at a higher volley. A deeper approach shot can also give you the ball you want. Deeper shots often cause "floating" returns that stay in the air longer as your opponent finds it difficult to get his body behind the ball to drive it. Maybe your opponent has not allowed you a chance to volley because he lobs you every time. Next time you approach the net, stop short of it at the service line. This will normally force your opponent away from the lob and give you a chance to volley.

If your opponent has been consistently hitting smooth strokes with a high margin for error and you want to see him miss just once, try moving him more. Often players with such control dislike having to hit on the run. This can force your opponent to hit a lower percentage shot and end the point earlier.

You have the potential to make your opponent hit the balls you want. Don't let your opponent play the shots *he* wants. Learn to play the shots to him that force him to hit the shots you desire him to play. You can, in essence, control the shots your opponent plays by making him hit the balls you want.

♀ CONTROL YOUR OPPONENT

The winner in a match will undoubtedly be the player who plays the game *his* way. He will be the one in control. This won't be indicated just in the score, but also in the way he controls his opponent.

Ball control ultimately means opponent control. If you are able to place the ball where you like and where your opponent dislikes, you will be in command. Your opponent might attempt a similar strategy by placing balls to your dislikes or weak strokes, and trying to get you to play the balls he likes. Exploit this strategy by playing the game *your* way. Be aware of his attempts and don't allow yourself to play to his game. Stay a step ahead of him to retain control.

Controlling the tempo, flow, and rhythm of a match can also help you control your opponent. The match will go according to your plans for it. If you want to slow it down, simply walk slower between points and take longer rests during the changeovers between games. If you'd like to keep the pace rapid, walk more quickly, take little or no rest between odd games, and begin your serve without hesitation each time.

I've watched some of the top players in the game like Connors, McEnroe, and Navratilova make their opponents look like rag dolls. They jerk them all over the court in complete control and move them like puppets on a string. They are obviously in control of the match because they have such control over their opponents.

ℚ *SUMMARY*

The best players are often the ones who don't appear impressive. They play effective shots that produce consistent results. The most determined player on the court is the usual victor. Focus your mind and motivate yourself with a stronger will and desire for victory. There are certain "big" points and crucial games in every match; learn to recognize and win them. Force your opponent to have an "off" day. Mix up your shots and break your opponent's rhythm with a variety of shots that he doesn't like. Learn to read your opponent's strokes and his mind. Good court sense is no more than a keen awareness of what your opponent is doing. Strengthen your mental game to gain the psychological advantage over your opponent. Play like a winner to be one. Make your opponent hit the balls you want. Learn to play your way to control your opponent and the match.

CHAPTER 5

Your Self-Image as a Tennis Player

✑ *GET TO KNOW YOURSELF*

Think for a moment on the image you have of yourself as a tennis player. Is the mental picture you have painted a good image, a bad one, or a fluctuating image of your abilities depending on your day-to-day play? It is very important for you to realize how you feel about yourself and your tennis abilities. These thoughts will become your limitations as a tennis player.

Have you ever known anyone with little self esteem to achieve much in life? They lack confidence in their abilities, so they have, in effect, limited themselves in what they can achieve. They usually won't attempt something that doesn't go along with the image they have of their capabilities. By the same token, if you don't think highly of yourself as a tennis player, you won't think to enter a higher level tournament. You can place yourself into a particular level in your mind, and will remain there until you change the way you think of yourself.

Your goals and aspirations as a tennis player depend on the limitations you set for yourself. Remember, *you can only achieve what you can conceive.* If you believe that you are capable of playing in the next higher level tournament, then you are probably ready to. Your image of yourself can be a powerful tool to help you improve your level of play.

The way you walk, talk, dress, and manage yourself are all determined by the person you believe yourself to be.

Someone with good thoughts of himself is seen in a better light by others. Be a confident player by painting a good image in your mind of your tennis abilities. If you don't ever paint that picture, you won't ever have the capability of becoming the player you'd like to be. A positive mental attitude is one of the most important ingredients necessary to realizing your tennis potential. Nothing can help improve your tennis game more.

℘ DEVELOPING YOUR CONFIDENCE

There is a big difference between a *confident* tennis player and a *conceited* one. A confident player is realistic about his abilities, while a conceited player has an exaggerated opinion of himself. Confidence in a player can be developed through a conditioning process of practice and belief. It requires building positive habits of thought in your mind and in your actions.

A confident tennis player feels good about himself even when his play might be inexcusable. He has a clear self image and believes in his abilities. He knows that he has performed well in the past and is capable of repeating these actions. He won't get angry with himself unless his confidence wavers.

Raising your level of confidence will undoubtedly raise your level of performance. Before you are relaxed enough to let go and play "in the zone," you must become a confident tennis player. Confidence can sometimes take time to develop in tennis. You must first believe in your strokes to be able to believe in your capacity to hit them well. This is why practice is so important in tennis. During this time, it is really more important to develop confidence in your strokes than it is to develop the strokes themselves. Once you are able to make a shot over and over your confidence will grow.

The best way I have found to develop confidence in tennis is to learn to feel good about your abilities in a "tie-breaker" situation. If you ever want to find out if someone is a confident tennis player, ask them if they like to play tie-breakers. This is the true test of ability because all the pressure is on — each point is a big point. If you can master a fair amount of success in winning tie-breakers, your confidence and your game can improve greatly.

If you think about it, there is never an opportune time

to lose a tie-breaker. If you reach six games all in the first set, you certainly don't want to lose the set after playing so hard to win six games. The thought of having to win an additional two sets should you lose the tie-breaker, never seems appealing at that moment either. How about losing a tie-breaker in the second or third set? If you lose the tie-breaker in the second set after having already lost the first, the match is over. Your struggles in the second set to even things up at one set each have fallen short. To win the tie-breaker would have put you back into the match. To lose a tie-breaker in the third set is what nightmares are made of! The horror of playing a long three-set match only to lose by a few points in the end should make you want to master the tie-breaker!

Developing your confidence requires that you practice your strokes and your positive mental thoughts of yourself and your actions. Don't be a conceited tennis player when you're really trying to develop your confidence. Have a positive but realistic image of yourself, and then believe in it. Since the game is filled with pressure situations and big points, put yourself under as many pressure and big point situations as possible to gain confidence in playing them. Learn to enjoy tie-breakers and let them help you to become the confident tennis player you desire to be.

♀ BELIEVE AND IT IS SO

Your future in tennis will mainly be decided by what you think and what you believe. The chief reason that players are beaten in tennis is that they believe they can be. You must believe that you will win if you ever hope to have a chance.

A winner is someone who believes he will win. He believes this until the final point of a match is played. If he finds himself down in a match, he overcomes the deficit through his strong conviction and refusal to accept defeat.

Many players have difficulties believing in themselves and their abilities. They are often content to play close or to take a set off of someone they regard as a good player. Their positive thoughts aren't high enough to allow them to leap over the hurdle of these close losses. They tell their friends that they have played close with someone respected as a good player in hope that they too will be regarded as a good player. They lack the necessary belief in themselves to win. Once the score reaches a point of contention in the player's mind, the match is really over.

All the great players in the game have believed that they would win and haven't been content until they did. Boris Becker could easily have been content with himself after reaching the Wimbledon semifinals for the first time. He proved, however, that he wasn't satisfied with simply a good showing, by proceeding to win the tournament at the age of seventeen. Most of the world didn't believe he could do it because they assumed he was too young and inexperienced to believe that he could.

A self-confident person is a believer. It is actually the belief that instills self confidence in a person. Learning to believe in yourself can help you develop your confidence and project your tennis game to new heights. If you believe that you're a player with the ability to excel, you will do just that. However, begin to doubt your abilities and watch your game stagnate. Believe you are prepared for the match and you will be. Believe that you will win and you won't allow defeat to happen.

⚲ ACT THE PART

People usually act like the people they think they are. Players who act like losers on the tennis court are usually the ones who will be. If you would like to be a winner, begin by acting like one!

You might need to become an actor to change your mental habits from negative into positive ones. Act as though you've already acquired the positive attitude and traits that you would like to have. This will require practice until you begin to really believe it. You can become a positive thinker and have the supreme self assurance you've wanted when you habitually act the part.

Tennis players are often seen at a tournament acting the part. Even though the tournament will produce only one winner in each division, you'll often see many players walking around like they've already won the event. Those players are sometimes referred to as "prima donnas" because of their cocky actions. They are merely trying to convince themselves that they will win by acting like they already have!

My advanced students always get a kick out of me telling them to strut around the house the week before an important match and convince themselves that "I'm gonna win!" This is not intended to be a boastful act. Instead it is intended to convince them that they will carry out the part they are acting.

Dr. Denis Waitley says in his "The Psychology of Winning" tapes that "people act not in accordance with reality, but in their perception of reality." You can make yourself believe whatever you want. Acting how you want to be is probably the best way to begin being who you want to be. First, picture in your mind the image of the tennis player you would like to be. Then begin acting like that player. Through practice you will believe, and will become the confident, winning player you've been portraying.

YOU'RE NOT ONLY AS GOOD AS YOUR SECOND SERVE, YOU'RE BETTER

If you want to demean yourself, simply pick out your worst stroke and dwell on it. This will surely make you think much less of yourself as a player.

Tennis professionals have often tried to stress the importance of a well-rounded game to their students by making such statements as, "Remember, you're only as good as your second serve." These are the players who crunch their first serves with all their might only to falter and then resort to a gentle push on their second serve to get the ball in play. Although the professionals' intentions were good, the results can sometimes be disastrous.

A well-rounded tennis game, played with comfortable and confident strokes, is essential to building a winning game. If there is a particular stroke you don't feel confident with, it is important to practice and improve it so your game will not suffer because of its inadequacies. But to allow your mind to continually harp on your weakest stroke will only lower your self-image, as you will believe that your are only as good as your weakest shot.

Everyone has both strong and weak strokes. It is important to recognize this, and to develop them into dependable strokes that you believe in. Often players spend much more time trying to improve their weaknesses than working on their strengths. If you're spending too much time improving your weak strokes, you might forget you have strengths! Not only do you want to practice your strengths to make them even better, you also want to practice them to remind yourself of your good points.

Something important to remember while you're practicing for your all-around game is that you want strokes that you will have confidence in. Talented players can often hit "all the shots in the book" but have trouble playing well day in and day out. Even though they can hit all the shots, they haven't the confidence in them to perform consistently. Practice your strokes to become confident with them. A limited number of strokes that you feel comfortable with can often be better than trying to master them all.

Regard yourself as a tennis player in terms of your strengths. Don't forget your weaknesses when it's time to improve them, but don't measure your ability by them. Refuse to let your mind dwell on your weaknesses. You're better than your second serve; don't convince yourself otherwise.

ᐤ PROGRAM YOUR MIND FOR SUCCESS

Your mind functions like a computer — you get back what you program in. If your thoughts are positive and confident of your ability as a tennis player, you'll believe in what you can do. If your thoughts tend to be negative and doubtful, you'll be programming self-defeat in your mind.

Success must first be conceived as a *mental reality* before it can become an *actual reality* in your performance. You must allow positive thoughts to enter your mind before success can be attained. In essence, you must think that you're capable of great accomplishments with your game before you can have the chance of actually achieving them.

Don't be afraid to think big thoughts about yourself and your tennis capabilities. Most players could become far better if they would only put their minds to it. Instead of thinking of bigger, more successful goals, the average player is too insecure with his faults and weaknesses to think beyond them. These players unknowingly spend most of their time programming their minds for defeat. After defeat sets in and becomes the norm, these are the same players who will begin to search for answers as to why they are losing!

Norman Vincent Peale says it best in his book, *The Amazing Results of Positive Thinking*: "Always act as if it were impossible to fail." Isn't this the way a winner focuses on success? They don't crowd their minds with self-defeating thoughts. They're too concerned with winning to worry about losing.

Keep a positive frame of mind and don't let minor setbacks defeat you. Everyone experiences mistakes and losses in the game, but winners won't let them affect their goal. They focus on success because they realize that this is how to bring out successful play in themselves.

℘ CAN'T IS A POWERFUL WORD

"Whether you think you can or you can't you're probably right." — Henry Ford.

Discipline yourself to refrain from using the word "can't" in describing your tennis abilities. It is one of the biggest self-defeating words in a tennis player's vocabulary. It means *can not* or simply, that you don't have the ability.

The word really is quite powerful. It sends a signal directly to your mind telling it not to attempt something, or that you know you're unable to do a particular task. As a teaching professional I can bear witness to the fact that once a student's mind has accepted defeat, it is like pulling teeth to get them to even attempt what they are saying they *can't* do.

You have learned how powerful belief can be earlier in this chapter. Once you say the word "can't," your mind believes it. It believes it because you wouldn't say it or think it unless you believed it, right? I'm sure you all know someone who has told a lie so long that he's convinced it is the truth. You can convince your mind that you really *can't* simply by repeating it over and over, just as the liar did until he was convinced that it was fact.

The converse of this also applies. If you repeat over and over that you *can* do something, your mind will respond by trying harder. It believes that it *can*, so it *will*. Learn to think positive thoughts so that your mind will not feel that it has limitations imposed on it. Make words such as "can" and other positive action words a habit in your vocabulary. You will discover that your mind will respond by believing in your abilities when you eliminate limiting thoughts.

♀ REMEMBER THE GOOD SHOTS

If you are perfectionist by nature, try not to be critical of yourself on the tennis court. Perfectionists like everything to be exact. They are very particular about the standards they set for themselves and for everything around them. If one little thing happens that is not according to plan, look for the perfectionist to get rattled.

When all goes well, perfectionists can be some of the most effective players in the game. However, the standards of a perfectionist are sometimes too strict or rigid. Often times the person becomes easily discontented, impatient, and too demanding with himself. He becomes self defeating by striving for something too ideal.

John McEnroe's court behavior can be attributed to his perfectionist traits. He has become a great player by striving for perfection in his game, but at the same time has been known to lose control of himself when everything doesn't go exactly as he'd like during a match.

Perfectionists play the game of tennis by hitting ten good shots and one poor one, only to dwell on the error until it brings them down mentally. A lowered self esteem is the result. Actually these players are probably playing quite well except that their minds are focusing on the negative, which will naturally bring them down.

The key to keeping yourself thinking positive and confident thoughts in a tennis match is not to dwell on your past mistakes. Even if you have perfectionist traits, you must remember that everyone makes errors in tennis and not to let them affect you negatively. Analyze your mistakes to learn why you erred, and then immediately correct the stroke in your mind. After you have mentally corrected the stroke, get the thought of the error out of your mind. Envision once again the good shots you've made. You will discover that it will be much easier to think positive thoughts and to keep a good mental picture of yourself playing well when you remember the good shots that you've hit and forget the bad ones.

♀ *COMPARE YOURSELF TO YOU*

Players often have low self esteem for their tennis game because they compare themselves to other players. These players to whom they compare themselves might possess greater tennis skills and abilities than they do, so it's automatically self defeating to compare to them. The same players who compare themselves to others also rarely take into account the amount of experience, preparation, and dedication their competitors have put into their games to result in such superior play.

It is always best to compare yourself only to YOU. In this regard, you will play within your own limitations and not those of someone else. A player who compares himself to others will try to hit all the shots his opponent can hit, not all the shots that he himself is capable of hitting. He plays the game without confidence because he is only imitating another person's game, not really playing his own.

Practice habits can also be best improved when you compare yourself only to you. It is always easier to watch the others at your club, and if they aren't working hard at their games, you needn't either. Instead, work hard at your game independently of what the others are doing. The benefits you will derive from practice are solely for you. You can become a self-motivated player when you stop looking to compare yourself with others.

Feel good about yourself as a tennis player. If you are honestly giving it your best, you should have a good image of yourself as a player. This good picture you are painting of yourself in your mind should be just that — *yourself.* Don't let someone else's image cloud the good thoughts you have of yourself.

♀ *SUMMARY*

Be a confident tennis player by painting a good image in your mind of your tennis abilities. Understand the difference between confidence and conceit. To develop confidence, have a positive but realistic image of yourself, and then *believe* in it. Develop a strong belief in yourself. Do this until the final point in every match that you play. To be a winner, start acting like one. Stop thinking of yourself in terms of your weaknesses. The image you have of yourself as a tennis player should be in terms of your strengths. Program positive thoughts into your mind for success. Replace the word "can't" with "can" in your vocabulary. Your mind believes what it is told, so choose positive action words carefully. Stop dwelling on the one error you've made until it brings you down. Remember all the good shots that you've hit to keep your self image positive. The person to compare yourself to as a player is *you*. See a clear image of yourself to develop your confidence and belief in your game.

CHAPTER 6

Prepare to Play Intelligently

♀ MENTALLY FIT

A physically fit person has a well-tuned body. Considerable time is usually spent conditioning it to bring it to this state of fitness. However, once a body is fit, it is then prepared to meet whatever physical challenge it might face. This same fitness can be applied to your mental state. With proper training and practice, you can condition your mind to be mentally fit.

Being a good player in practice but falling apart in a match shows a need to get your mind mentally fit. Players who suffer concentration problems in a match are usually the very ones who neglect the proper mental preparation. Rarely, if ever, will they practice concentration, handling of pressure, or intensity. To produce a high level of concentration consistently requires proper conditioning and training of the mind. Your quality of readiness will be directly related to how well you practiced and prepared your mind for the match.

It is very important to be in the right frame of mind to play an intelligent game of tennis. Feeling good about yourself and your game can help you have the best possible attitude before the match begins. Your confidence will develop as you believe you are mentally fit and prepared. This can enable you to relax your body and let go during the match to play in the ideal mental state: "in the zone."

Feeling comfortable with your ability to remain in control

Jogging is a great way to build your conditioning and stamina for tennis.

can ease the tension you might experience before a match. A mind that is in control of emotions will be clear to focus all the attention on the task at hand. Sharpen your mind by adjusting your intensity level to produce a greater attention span and to develop a keen awareness of what you are about to do. Being mentally fit means you are prepared for the task at hand and are in control of yourself and your mental state.

♀ PHYSICALLY ABLE

Most tennis players play the game to stay in shape, never attempting to play their best by getting into shape first. When you are physically prepared, you feel like you have the "edge." This feeling of being physically fit will strengthen your confidence and positive attitude about yourself going into a match.

Physical conditioning is something that can easily get pushed aside in the priorities you set for your daily life. If you truly have the desire to play the best tennis you are capable of, commit yourself to get in the best shape you possibly can. Discipline yourself to shed those extra pounds you are carrying which inhibit you from reaching all shots on the court. Reaching just one extra ball that you've been unable to get could help you to win many extra points.

Try to discover the means that will help you produce a fitter body. John McEnroe prefers to just play more tennis, so he enters more tournaments and even plays in all the doubles so that he can stay physically sharp. Martina Navratilova prepares for her matches by playing little tennis but lots of basketball to keep her body fit. She also works with weights to build her stamina and strength.

Your diet can also have an influence on your game. It can help maximize your potential and performance. Many professional athletes stick to diets such as those recommended by Robert Haas, Ph.D. Their diets consist primarily of carbohydrates, which are digested rapidly but supply a great source of energy to the athlete. These foods include whole grain cereals and breads, brown rice, fresh fruit, pasta, and potatoes. They stay away for large amounts of protein in their pre-game meals because high protein foods are digested slowly and are a poor source of energy.

Take the time to get into shape to play tennis. You'll discover that not only will you enjoy playing a better game of tennis, you'll also feel better and more confident about yourself and your abilities. Discipline yourself to make your physical conditioning an important part of your preparation to play an intelligent game of tennis.

♀ GROOVED STROKES

The time to get all of the "bugs" worked out of your strokes is when you are *preparing* to play a match. You don't want to have tentative strokes on your mind once the match begins. This is when your mind needs to be clear and focused on other relevant actions in the match. Be analytical of your strokes before the match and not during it.

Prepare your confidence in yourself by feeling comfortable with your strokes prior to the match. Get your strokes grooved into sync by feeling good about your timing of the ball. Feel the ball stay on the strings longer and practice your control over the ball and its direction.

Sometimes repetition is required to gain belief in your strokes. A ball machine can serve the useful purpose of helping you groove your strokes. A drill partner can also help you gain confidence in your strokes by feeding repeated shots to you until your strokes feel comfortable. Serves shouldn't be neglected either as you prepare your strokes for playing an intelligent match. Get a basket of balls and practice the depth and placement of your hits. This is the time to get the kinks out of our serve if you aren't totally confident with it.

As you are preparing your strokes, don't forget to include a few emergency situations in your drills so that you will be prepared for them when they occur in a match. This might include a session of balls coming to you where you aren't expecting them, or shots that are mixed up at a variety of speeds and spins. Again, use this time to analyze errors and try to correct your mistakes so that you will have a better understanding of them during match play. Develop a general confidence in yourself and your strokes by letting them "feel good" before the match begins.

✐ *TIPS TO REMEMBER*

In a match situation, it is important not to crowd your mind with technical jargon on your strokes and play. This can easily break your concentration even though you may only be trying to find a way to play better. The simplest way to do this is to make a quick analysis of your error or to offer your mind a reminder of the correct focus for a particular stroke. This can be accomplished by learning a shortened "tip" that you can use to analyze errors and reprogram the focus of your mind during a match. This is the most efficient and effective way to keep your concentration on the match but remain aware of what you are doing.

Listed below are a number of tips that I like to use. You may use these, or you may want to make up your own set of tips to use while playing.

- "Hit through the ball"...better ball control
- "Squeeze the grip before contact"...firmer shots
- "Think two nets"...better net clearance
- "Feel the ball"...better ball control
- "Go to the ball"...aggressive play
- "Quick feet, slow racket"...smooth strokes
- "Lengthen the contact"...better ball control
- "Push the palm on forehands"...to hit through the ball
- "Why did the ball go there?"...stroke analysis
- "Don't hit the ball, guide it"...better ball control
- "Hit up, not down"...better stretch and net clearance on serves
- "Catch ball"...little racket movement on volleys
- "Hit seven balls instead of one"...better ball control
- "Eyes and ball same level"...bend with volleys
- "Pass with ease, not with power"...to avoid rushed passing shots
- "Aim a yard from the line"...good margin for error
- "Every shot has a target"...to stop aimless hitting
- "Throw racket to a cloud"...hitting up for better serves
- "Clean a shelf"...high ground strokes
- "Reach up, snap down"...power on serves
- "Fall forward"...to volley more in front
- "Errors are how you win points"...percentage tennis
- "Let the racket do the work"...power on serves
- "Back to the basics"...when all feeling is gone on strokes

- "Contact in front of knees"...take ball early/avoid late contacts
- "Lift those groundstrokes"...better net clearance
- "Match effort to the task"...when you're over-hitting or using too much energy
- "Arm and racket together"...avoid wristy shots
- "Line up your body"...better footwork and positioning

⚲ READY FOR ALL CONDITIONS

Rarely will all conditions be perfect while you're playing a match. Ideal playing situations occur so infrequently because it is difficult to have the temperature just right, not too much sunshine, the right amount of wind, a perfect bounce, and an opponent who hits all shots that you can play. Since it is so rare that everything is perfect, why do most players only practice and prepare as if it were going to be perfect?! Practice playing on a variety of tennis courts with different surfaces. Play in all kinds of weather to know what to expect. Practice playing at night on occasion. Practice with a variety of tennis players to prepare yourself for the many different styles of play.

Tennis balls behave differently on different court surfaces. It is important to prepare your strokes according to the different bounce. Any player who does not have a clear understanding of this and who has not spent the necessary time practicing for these different bounces will be in for quite a surprise. The ball will bounce lower and quicker on smooth court surfaces, such as those found on grass or older hard courts. The more textured a court surface is, the slower and higher the bounce of the ball will be. These are often the traits of clay courts, newer hard courts, and some synthetic surface courts. Being able to properly adjust the preparation and timing of your strokes is essential for you to play a comfortable game on the various court surfaces.

Weather can also be a major factor in the outcome of a match. Players must learn to accept the conditions and adjust their games to them if they hope to succeed playing in ever-changing weather conditions. Look forward to practicing on days when it is windy, hot and sunny, cold, humid, and drizzling to be prepared should any of these conditions occur on an important match day.

Skip is ideally positioned to "catch the ball" on his racket for a controlled volley.

Certain styles of players can also ruin your hopes for an ideal match situation if you aren't prepared for them. Practice against left handers, two-handed players, big hitters, pushers, big spinners, and chop artists to be ready for all types of players.

Your quality of preparation will be based on *how* and *what* you practiced. If your practices are limited only to ideal situations (i.e., practice only when the weather is just right and you have the perfect partner to hit with), then how do you expect to be prepared for the ever-changing conditions you will face? Be ready for spectators who might be watching during your match and outside noises that might occur while you're playing. Check your equipment to make sure it is in good condition and will offer no surprises once the match begins. It will be much easier to control situations if you're ready for them. The players who aren't will often find the situations controlling them. Your confidence and self control will be directly related to how prepared you are to meet and handle the various conditions and situations you'll face in a match.

♀ KNOW YOUR LIMITATIONS

The best way to be prepared for a match is to practice as you would play. Get "your game" ready for the match by practicing and strengthening your confidence in the game you plan to use.

To understand your game, get to know your strengths and weaknesses. Be aware of your capabilities before you attempt shots that you can't execute. This is the first step to developing your own game style. Learn to play *within yourself.*

Professional tennis players have reached their level of play by realizing their limitations and playing within them. Chris Evert has been a champion for years because she plays the game that she knows she is capable of. Even though she has been one of the top tennis players on the women's tour for many years, that doesn't mean that she can hit any shot, any time she likes. She knows her game and her limitations and plays her game within them.

Errors are often made in a match when players attempt shots they shouldn't. Strokes that they aren't able to execute consistently become a challenge to them. Often they will continue to attempt these shots instead of learning what they are best at and playing those shots most often. Remember, errors are how points are won in a tennis match, so prepare your game within your own limitations to reduce the number of errors you will make.

⚹ THE GAME PLANS

Tennis, like all sports, requires a game plan in order to win. Other sports often have a staff of coaches who work together to decide the way the team needs to play in order to win the game. They review films of their opponents and send out scouts to monitor and watch their every move. You need to use this same strategy to get a better understanding of the opposition before you begin playing a tennis match. Discover their likes and dislikes and learn what shots they prefer in different match situations. If you are unable to scout your opponent beforehand, ask someone who might know them as many questions as you can relating to this person's game. The information you receive can help you tremendously in formulating the proper game plan to use.

Other factors to consider when planning your match strategy include the court surface the match will be played on, as well as any other pertinent conditions that might affect the way you will play the match. For example, if the court is a textured surface such as clay which produces a slow, high-bouncing ball, you should consider this when planning how you will play. If your game normally relies on quick rallies with you ending the point in a hurry, you might want to adopt a new strategy for playing on this type of surface. What is most important is to practice on the court surface that your match will be played on before the match begins. That way you will be familiar with the way it plays and, above all, you can learn to like it!

It is important to map out several game plans in case your first one fails. For example, Plan A might be comprised of your favorite play — aggressive style; your opponent's weaknesses — backhand and handling of pressure; and the court surface — fast hard court. In this plan, your strategy is to attack and keep the pressure on your opponent by coming in behind serves, attacking his second serves and all short balls. If Plan A should falter and you find yourself behind by enough of a margin to change gears, Plan B or C should be implemented. Plan B or C could be as drastic a change as becoming totally defensive and staying back on the baseline for all points, or it could be a slight change such as altering only the frequency and timing of your attack.

Be prepared with alternatives should your favorite style of play not be the correct game to use, or should you discover that your opponent's assumed weaknesses are actually his strengths! Your strategy for the match will be formulated by an accumulation of information on your game and its limitations, your opponent's game, the court surface of the match, and other conditions which can affect the overall outcome of the match. Be flexible in preparing your game plans. You might have to adopt an entirely different strategy than you've planned if it becomes necessary in the match.

✐ THINK TENNIS

In the days preceding a match, get your mind more in focus on *tennis*. Players often think that their minds can click on and off at will and thus neglect to properly prepare their minds by "thinking tennis" prior to the match.

To immediately turn off the thoughts that consume your everyday life, and to turn on the thoughts of tennis when it's time is no easy task. Allow your mind an easier transition by making tennis a part of your thoughts prior to playing. Read a tennis book or magazine or watch a tennis match. It can help to keep your mind enthused and excited about the game.

Practice can even be done in your mind in preparation for playing. Your mind can simulate match situations and visualize playing points in your thoughts. This can be done over and over in your mind, just as you would hit a forehand over and over in practice. Get your mind in tune to tennis before the match. Your concentration and mental focus can be improved during match play by "thinking tennis" long before the match ever begins.

♀ FIND YOUR ROUTINE

Pre-match preparation should be as individualized as your personal needs and preferences. This is because it must be whatever makes you comfortable, confident, and ready to play the match to the best of your ability. It might require experimentation if you haven't established a routine for yourself, however, finding a routine is vital to complete your match preparation.

When should you arrive for the match? What and when should you eat? How much sleep should you have the night before? What physical activity should you do prior to the match? Should you stretch? Should you hit? How long? These are questions that you will need to answer in order to establish a suitable routine.

I'd like to offer some general guidelines for you to consider which might prove helpful in finding your routine. Plan to arrive early. Warm up, if possible, to break a sweat and relieve a little of your nervous tension. Try to hit a variety of strokes as you would in a match. Get a good feeling of the ball on all strokes. Stretch to relax the muscles in your body after you have *finished* the warmup. Players are often seen stretching their cold bodies *before* the warmup which can cause injury. The best example is comparing it to trying to stretch cold salt water taffy. Taffy will only stretch when warm, and will break when it's cold.

You should always try to allow enough time before your match for the food you've eaten to digest, say one and a half to two hours. This will help you avoid feeling bloated and immobile on the court during play. Your diet should consist primarily of carbohydrates.

Your sleeping pattern probably shouldn't be adjusted if you awake invigorated and ready for the day. If you often waken feeling sluggish or tired, you might want to allow extra time for sleep to feel good and rested on match day.

In your routine, allow yourself enough time for mental preparation. This will be the time to sharpen the focus of your mind by relaxing your body and clearing your mind of all anxieties and tensions. This is one of the most crucial parts of a good routine, but one that is often neglected. Rid your mind of all the thoughts that are clouding it, and refocus your thoughts on the match at hand. You are now ready and prepared to play your best.

⚲ SUMMARY

Practicing well but falling apart in matches shows the need to become mentally fit. Condition your mind to prepare for match situations by strengthening your concentration in practice. Discipline yourself to get into shape to play better tennis. Not only will you enjoy playing better, but you'll also feel better and more confident of yourself and your tennis abilities. Prepare by feeling comfortable with your strokes prior to match play. Analyze and correct your strokes *before* the match so that you won't have them on your mind while you're playing. To avoid clouding your mind with analytical thoughts of your game during the match, learn some quick tips. These can be an efficient and effective way to keep you aware of what you are doing, as well as keeping your mind clear to allow for good concentration.

Rarely will all conditions be perfect for a match, so stop practicing as it they were going to be. Your quality of preparation will be based on how and what you practiced. Get to know your game along with your strengths and weaknesses. Understand your limitations and learn to play within them. It is important to have several game plans for the match. Let your mind be prepared for the transition of thinking only on tennis during your match by "thinking tennis" more often in the days prior to playing. Find a routine that you feel comfortable and confident with. Your pre-match habits are a vital part of your preparation to play an intelligent game of tennis.

CHAPTER 7

Playing an Intelligent Match

♀ *PLAY YOUR OPPONENT'S SHOTS, NOT HIS NAME*

So many matches will be won or lost before they ever begin because of self doubt or overconfidence. This happens most often to players without them ever realizing what they are doing to themselves and their chances of success in a match. The most important thing to remember is that *your opponent is only as good as he is that day!*

I've noticed that many of my students will play differently against players who have reputations of being "really good players." It won't necessarily be because of the shots that these players hit, but rather it's the name and reputation of these players which causes the change in their style of play. They are in effect "psyched out" and would probably be content to play a close match with these players, since they have no thoughts of ever beating them.

Put your opponent's reputation, good or bad, out of your mind. Play each match as a "fresh start" where both of you have to prove yourselves. Play the shots that your opponent hits, and forget about his name. Remember that he will only be as good as the day you play him. This also holds true for players you expect to beat easily. Don't let overconfidence spoil your chances of victory. You never know how your opponent will play until the match actually begins.

℺ WIN THE WARMUP

Matches can be won or lost in the warmup. This short period when you and your opponent have the first opportunity to hit just before playing the match is an important one. Use this time wisely and avoid taking a casual approach to loosen yourself up. Get your body and your mind in tune. Let your opponent know from your actions that you're tough, determined, and focused on winning.

As you begin hitting with your opponent, give the impression of being cool, deliberate, and confident. Relax and don't feel rushed with your strokes or your movement. Get your strokes feeling right with good ball control and placement. Be emotionally unconcerned about your errors or his superb play. Focus your mind on the task and be keenly aware of what you are doing.

Analyze your opponent's strokes, movement, strengths, and weaknesses. Give him a wide variety of shots to test his ability to hit them. Vary the pace, depth, spin, and placement to experiment with his capabilities. Read your opponent by noticing what he does with his racket, shoulders, feet, and body movements on each shot. Look to develop your anticipation in the match by reading how he hits his different strokes to different places on the court. Any signals that you can pick up on will help you tremendously in your ability to be in the right place at the right time during the match.

Mix up your shots in the warmup, not only to test your opponent's ability to handle the variety of shots, but also to prevent him from getting grooved. This is possible to do and still remain sportsmanlike in the process. In this manner, you will create an insecurity in your opponent as he will be less sure of the strokes he will hit going into the match. This is exactly the tactic to use once the match begins, so use the warmup to set the tone of your control over the match.

℺ FIRST IMPRESSIONS ARE LASTING

Do your best to avoid slow starts in every match you play. This is a powerful impression that shouldn't be overlooked. It is a known fact that first impressions are influential and lasting. Wouldn't it then be logical that how you appear and play at the beginning of each match would be of utmost importance? This is the first impression you make on your opponent!

Slow starters tend to play long matches. They usually neglect to prepare and use the warmup wisely, so they often need to get grooved the first few games in the match. They make senseless errors at the beginning of a match as they "hit out" to feel the ball, and often find themselves down and being controlled by their opponent right from the start.

Sharpen your mental state and control your actions to make them deliberate and confident. Begin the match by playing a high percentage game of tennis that allows a high margin for error on all shots. Your opponent will also be nervous at the beginning of the match, and letting him start out with a lead will only make him more comfortable and relaxed with his play. *Keep the ball in play* and strive to make as few errors at the beginning of the match as you possibly can. By doing this you will never afford your opponent the opportunity to get comfortable with his play. He'll get himself behind by making all the errors first.

How you look and act at the onset of a match will stay in your opponent's mind. Appear cool, unconcerned, and in control. How you begin hitting will also signal your focused determination as you strive to hit controlled balls with confident swings. Your consistency and the steadiness of your play will make a lasting impression in your opponent's mind. I've seen many, many players "fold" in the beginning of matches when their opponents appeared invincible. Get on top early to establish your determination and control. Let your first impression be that you are in control of the ball, yourself, your opponent, and the match. This is one powerful signal that will surely last in the mind of your opponent.

CONTROL THE TEMPO OF THE MATCH

Take control of the match by establishing the momentum of play. The match will either go at your pace, your opponent's pace, or no one's pace. It depends entirely on who wants to take control of it!

Control of the tempo of the match is important to enable

you to feel comfortable with the pace at which you play. As a general rule of thumb, speed up the play if you are in the lead, and slow it down if you find yourself behind. In both cases, by controlling the tempo of the match you can control the momentum of play.

Advanced players understand how to control a match by rushing or forcing their opponents. In this way they are said to "get on top of their opponents, and stay on top of them." They keep the momentum in their favor and are able to close out the matches that they play much more easily. The momentum in tennis is known to change frequently, so those who have learned to control it have a definite advantage. If you've played competitive tennis, I'm sure that you've experienced times when you were on top of your opponent and let up, only to find the momentum shift and yourself start to lose.

Slow the game down should you begin losing control over the match, much as you would if you were driving an uncontrollable car. Walk more slowly and take more time between points and odd game changeovers. Let your opponent's impetus dwindle as you slowly take control of the tempo of the match. Make your opponent play the game at the pace you set, and look to control the momentum of the match should it swing your opponent's way.

♀ BE A COURT GENERAL

Growing up in a military family, I'm well accustomed to the leadership role that officers in the service have over their men (and their sons). They are usually "take charge" people and have a "gutsy" attitude in the performance of their jobs. They are leaders because they are determined in their decision making and confident in their quest. Remember General Patton? He was known as a fierce field leader who wasn't afraid to take total control of every situation he found himself in!

To play tennis as a "court general" requires you to take charge of your actions and be responsible for them on the tennis court. Fight with a gutsy attitude by recognizing your opponent's weaknesses and capitalizing on them. Use the element of surprise by playing the balls your opponent doesn't like, when he least expects it. Keep him guessing with ever-changing strategies that bewilder him. Use intelligence and courage to adapt your game and keep your opponent off balance.

A good court general knows never to change a winning game, and that he must change a losing one. As the match progresses, he is aware of every situation and is ready to adjust his game plan accordingly should the need arise. If he has begun the match assuming that his opponent's backhand was the weaker stroke, he won't be afraid to begin playing to his opponent's forehand should he find himself trailing in the match. He takes positive corrective action without hesitation and moves forward with the new plan of attack.

Even though a court general is always thinking, he is doing so on his tactics and not necessarily on his strokes. He is making conscious decisions, but his actions on the court are still unconscious in nature because of the firm confidence that he holds in himself. He leads himself to victory because of his intense determination and desire as well as his superior tactical mind.

⚲ PRESSURE YOUR OPPONENT

Tennis matches are filled with pressure situations. Although pressure can help you to perform your best if you learn how to handle it properly, few players like to be put into pressure situations because they practice handling it so rarely. They would prefer to avoid it rather than learn to face it. To most, pressure situations represent a state of panic or disarray. Since this is true of most players, strive to put the pressure on your opponent in the match before he has the opportunity to put it on you!

So many situations in a match can be called "pressure" situations. Pressure mounts when it is a "must perform" situation. An example might be every time you get the ball back over the net, your opponent has the pressure placed on him to hit it back over. If you charge the net or force your opponent to hit a shot he isn't comfortable with, the pressure for him to perform is that much more increased.

Pressure your opponent in a match by charging the net if he doesn't like to have you up there, or by keeping the balls deep to him if he can't handle them there, or by hitting a harder-paced ball than he likes to play. It is playing his dislikes and forcing him to play a game he isn't comfortable with that creates a pressure situation in his mind. Other pressure situations you can create for him are those where you appear infallible. When you keep all the balls coming back, keep getting a high percentage of your first serves in, and return all of his serves back, he will feel pressured to produce better and better shots in order to win.

The score of the match can also place pressure on your opponent. Always try to establish the lead in each game by winning the first point and all those when the point score is even, such as fifteen-all or deuce. Winning the first game and all games when the score is even also keeps the pressure on your opponent as he must attempt to rally from behind.

There are many "clutch" moments in a match where the pressure might be on both of you. Concentrate on winning those key points to always shift the pressure to your opponent. You can play a more relaxed game of tennis when you learn to keep the pressure off of yourself by applying it to your opponent.

♀ VISUALIZE YOUR SHOTS

All shots in tennis should be hit with a target in mind. What is often lacking with uncontrollable strokes is a specific target. Body and racket preparation along with stroke execution all should occur only after a target is first conceived in the mind.

The two most important strokes in the game, the serve and the return of serve, could be greatly improved by the use of *visualization*. Visualization occurs when you look at your desired target, and in your mind "think the stroke there." Visually go through in your mind hitting the ball smoothly to your target. For both the serve and the return, there is a period of time prior to the stroke that will allow you the chance to prepare to hit the ball where you want by visualizing it there.

Visualization is not a method of producing shots beyond your skill level. It isn't about dreaming or fantasizing about unbelievable shots that you might hit. It is simply seeing in advance, in your mind, the shot you would like to play. Repeat the visions in your mind prior to executing the stroke as necessary until you're focused on them. This will help direct your mind to the desired target as well as program your mind for execution of the stroke.

Visualization can also aid your confidence if you should find yourself trailing in a match. See yourself back in control and playing well. Envision your comeback and charge yourself up to enact the command. Let your mind see a vision of success in your strokes and game.

Visualization helps program your thoughts in a focused manner. Your mind will have clearer directions to your desired targets, and you will discover that execution of your strokes will be an easier task. Think your strokes to your targets, and let your mind help you to play a better game of tennis.

⚲ LET GO AND LET IT HAPPEN

Players who have done their homework and properly prepared for a match are ready to anticipate the game situations, have made realistic game plans, believe in themselves and their strokes, have their minds focused on the match, and are ready to let go and let it all happen. To be able to reach this ideal playing state requires a relaxed body, free from tension, and a mind that is sharp and in control.

Try to keep your mind in focus on the moment. Don't let it wander, especially at idle times such as those between points. Absorb yourself with the match and get all of your thoughts to center on a keen awareness of what you are doing. Your attitude and spirits should, above all, be positive.

Confidence and belief in your abilities are the most vital ingredients to being able to "let go." Players who find themselves tight or tense during match play are usually insecure about something that is taking place. To be completely relaxed and free to let go and have your mind take over will require a belief in your strokes, yourself, and your mind and its abilities. Players who have experienced playing "in the zone" or in automatic have said that they played their best tennis ever in this state. You can consistently reach this level by learning to let go and let it happen.

ℚ MAKE INTELLIGENT ERRORS

Errors can be reduced in match play by simply playing shots that offer a higher margin for error. However, eliminating all errors in a match is an impossible task since tennis players are human and therefore imperfect. Even the top players in the world can be seen making errors during *every* match that they play. They usually don't make quite as many as the average club player does. They have learned to make *intelligent errors* when they miss, as opposed to simply making a mistake like the players who play with their minds turned "off" do.

The professionals play intelligently by being aware of what they are doing and correcting all of their mistakes immediately in their minds. They might be seen making a different mistake trying to correct the first one, but *rarely will they make the same mistake over and over again.*

A good example of an intelligent error is what I like to call an "Intelligent Double Fault." This might occur when a server has hit the first ball into the net and misses the second serve long over the service line. It was intelligent because he was aware of his mistake (hitting the ball into the net), and corrected it by directing the ball higher, only to miss long.

A typical player might hit seven or eight serves into the net and say to himself, "Boy, my serve sure has left me." No awareness is present as to *where* he is directing the ball or *how* to correct it. He simply reasons that he has made an error and his serve is "off." This is unintelligent tennis play at its worst. What is off is the player's mind, not his stroke!

To be an intelligent player requires a sharp mind and a keen awareness of what is taking place. Faults should be observed and corrected without passing judgment on them. Be in tune to every point. Players who have mental lapses of three to four points without realizing what they are doing, where the mistakes are being made, and why they are making them are simply going through the motions. Their minds aren't focused on what is happening and the result is unintelligent play!

Attempt to reduce your errors to play an intelligent match. If you must err, learn from it to avoid making the same mistakes again and again. Analyze your mistakes in your mind immediately after you've made them to reprogram your mind for corrective action. Then relax your body and focus your attention on the match. Dwelling on past mistakes and anger will only bring you down mentally. Nothing can be learned from such negative actions, and further progress in the game is hopeless unless errors are analyzed and corrected.

⚲ REMEMBER THE BASICS

Players who have a good understanding and have built their games on a solid foundation of the basics can never really be in trouble with their strokes. If all else fails, they need only to remember "go back to the basics."

This is a very secure feeling to have. Connors, Rosewall, Laver, and the other great champions of the game have all felt confident about their play because even if they experienced an off day, they knew they could fall back on the basics to keep their strokes form falling apart.

Beginners to top-ranked club players alike should learn a lesson from these great champions. Developing confidence in your game and performing well consistently requires a good working knowledge of the basics of the game. Ball control and how to increase it are the most important basics to fall back on. Keep the ball on the strings a little longer and "feel" the ball better for increased control. Direct the ball by hitting *through it* to the desired target. Strive for quality of ball control such as power, spins, and depth only after you feel comfortable with your ability to direct the ball where you want.

Another basic to remember is to hit shots that offer a higher margin for error. It is your errors that win the points for your opponent. Play a game of tennis that matches the efforts of your stroke to the task. Hit efficient and effective shots that get the job done, instead of flashy shots intended to look good, but often lacking consistency. Concentrate on holding serve, and mix up your shots to your opponent's dislikes to make him play the game you desire.

Feel free to turn back and reread Chapter 1, Understanding the Basics. A solid foundation needs to be built from your understanding and application of these basics of the game. Confidence and security can be instilled in your game once you feel comfortable with a working knowledge of the basics. Without this solid base to fall back on, your tennis game is destined for a rough-and-tumble roller coaster ride of highs and lows.

ℚ *PLAY LIKE A WINNER*

Have you ever noticed the difference in the way a loser plays a match as opposed to how a winner plays it? There is usually an obvious difference in the way winners and losers play. Not only does the winner generally control the match, but he also *looks* like he's winning.

A winner appears confident and in control by the way that he walks and carries himself around the court. His head is not down with slumping shoulders, nor does he drag his feet around like a disgusted child.

A loser normally plays a game called "desperate tennis." Once he finds himself behind in the match, he attempts to come back by taking more risks and trying to hit more outright winners with his strokes. The result is even lower percentage play as he attempts shots with a very low margin for error. While he is trying so hard to produce these difficult shots, his strokes appeared more forced than natural. This usually creates rushed or hectic swings with less "feel" for the ball and less control over it.

A winner on the other hand, doesn't have to play desperate tennis because he has the lead. He can be relaxed and confident and let his strokes flow smoothly and naturally. His concentration is not on forcing low percentage shots, but rather on playing shots which allow a high margin for error. This strategy keeps the momentum in his favor by making his opponent continue to play desperately.

You can decide to play like a winner whenever you want to, as it makes no difference whether you're winning or losing in the match. Losers could play like winners if only they decided to, but so often they appear content with not thinking beyond their losing status. Winners have been known to lose their lead when they forget to play like they're winning. Maybe they're so used to playing "desperate tennis" that they find it hard to play like a winner once they find themselves in the lead!

Relax and be confident. Let your strokes flow naturally. Think that you will win and believe it until the final point has been played. Stay away from playing "desperate tennis" and learn to play like a winner, no matter what the score is. You'll discover it much easier to become the winner when you learn to play like one!

⚲ SUMMARY

Your opponent is only as good as he is the day you play him. Put your opponent's reputation, good or bad, out of your mind and play his shots, not his name. Use the warmup to your advantage in the match. Test your opponent on his ability to handle a variety of shots. Do your best to avoid starting slowly in every match. First impressions are powerful, and how you begin will send a lasting signal of your abilities to your opponent. The momentum in tennis changes frequently in a match. Those who have learned to control it have a definite advantage over their opponents.

Be a "court general" and lead yourself to victory with determination and a gutsy attitude. Adjust your game plan as the match progresses by taking positive corrective action without hesitation, and moving forward with the new plan. Keep the pressure on your opponent throughout the match. Make him feel like nothing is going well with his strokes and that he must constantly play from behind in the match. Hit your shots to the desired targets through the use of visualization. Think your shots there by programming your mind with clear and focused directions.

Through confidence and belief in your abilities, let go and let it happen during the match. If you must make a mistake, make it an intelligent one. Be aware of what you are doing and make immediate corrections in your mind so you won't repeat the same mistakes. Go back to the basics should all else fail during the match. Play like a winner no matter what the score is. You'll discover it is much easier to become one!

CHAPTER 8

Develop an Enthusiasm for Learning

⚲ *ABOUT ENTHUSIASM*

"Nothing great was ever achieved without enthusiasm." — Ralph Waldo Emerson.

Have you noticed the enthusiasm that a child has for learning? Everything seems to be a source of joy and fascination to them. They get a tremendous thrill out of what seem to be the most ordinary things in life. From seeing and learning new games for the first time to their first bicycle ride, they are truly thrilled. As children mature, however, their enthusiasm for learning usually becomes dulled as the newness of most things wears off.

Beginning tennis players sometimes have a similar enthusiasm for learning the game. Everything is so fresh and new and there is so much to learn. As they mature as tennis players often their enthusiasm wears off, as does their desire to learn. What might happen is that they find themselves stuck on a plateau, unable to reach the next highest level. They lack the enthusiasm to obtain more knowledge of the game.

Enthusiasm is the key that can change the mental outlook of a situation. It is a positive emotion that can arouse a charge of energy in the person inspired with it. The mind is more eager and open to learn when enthusiasm is present.

Get the excitement of learning back into your thoughts! Crave the knowledge of the game that you might be missing. Seek to understand that game of tennis as if it were a brave, new, unexplored world. In this way you will continue learning, as your thoughts keep everything new and fresh. However, when you've lost your enthusiasm, your desire to learn slowly fades and so does your tennis game.

ᐁ *GENERALITIES WILL GET YOU NOWHERE*

I grew up playing competitive tennis with a pretty feisty attitude but with little sense. After every match that I lost I could always be heard saying, "I should have won." Although this statement in itself isn't so bad, my thoughts about the match usually ended there. It took my practical-minded father, who isn't a tennis player, to say, "Well, why didn't you?" This forced me to start getting specific, and to begin looking for the answers.

The answers to all your tennis problems will only come when you get *specific*. General thoughts and statements about your play will never get you anywhere.

Tennis players love to use generalities to explain themselves. Statements such as: "I played bad today." "My serve was off." "My forehand was terrible." "My backhand was the pits." "My opponent was too good." "My volley missed every time." "Nothing went right." "I lost."

To learn to be more specific, try placing the word "why" after every general statement as many times as needed to come up with the solution. An example of how you might find the specific answer to your backhand could be as follows: "My backhand was the pits. Why? All of them went long. Why? I don't know. Why?" You've now discovered where the problem lies; you're hitting your backhand long, but you are unsure as to specifically why it happened. Consult a qualified teaching professional to uncover the reason you backhand goes long or search for the answer yourself.

Only when you have specific answers can you begin to learn from them. Players who choose to generalize are making the choice not to learn. It is safer to generalize because it's always a much easier picture to see. It's more difficult to dig deep and get specific. Looking for the easy way out is only human nature. Don't let this happen to you! It's the more difficult things that you do in life that are the most worthwhile! To continue learning about the game, look for specifics to find the answers. Most players could greatly improve their games if only they would try to understand *why* they were winning or losing the points.

ꊦ *A CLEAR UNDERSTANDING*

A complete understanding of *how* you won or lost is the most important lesson in learning more about the game. It is so vital, yet so rarely emphasized.

Judging your strokes and play following a match really isn't what matters. What is important is an *understanding* of what took place. Play the match over in your mind and try to find out what happened, both good and bad. Try to be as specific as possible. Remember where your errors were made, and learn what caused them to occur. Look not only for the physical mistakes but also for the mental ones. Hopefully, you were able to make the necessary corrections during the match and avoid making repeated errors. If you weren't able to recognize and correct your errors during the match, take the time after the match to replay them in your mind. Learn to recognize what you are doing and why.

The Germans have a saying, *"All ist Klear?"* It means "Is everything clear?" If something is not clear, you won't have a total understanding of it. If your understanding of the match isn't clear, ask yourself questions to discover answers. Did you give 100%? Did you have good control of the ball? Were you patient? Were you relaxed? Was your mind focused clearly? Were your strokes smooth? Were you in control of yourself? Were your strokes hit with good margin for error? Ask as many questions as necessary to find a better understanding of what actually happened.

There is always a *reason* for your wins and losses. Search for it to gain the knowledge of yourself and your game. It takes intelligence to learn from your play, and it is senseless not to!

ꊦ *DO AN INDIVIDUAL, MATCH, AND OPPONENT ANALYSIS*

Sometimes a clearer picture is easier when it's written in black and white, and is before your eyes to see. A good way to help you better understand your play is to have your match "charted." Ask a friend or someone watching your match to record the points that you win as well as those you lose on a sheet of paper called an "Individual Evaluation Chart." (A sample chart is on page 118.)

Top-ranking college and professionals' coaches use this method to let their players see *where* the mistakes and points are being won and lost. It is a helpful tool to aid in the learning process of match play tennis. At the end of the match you will be able to look at the chart and see the errors made as well, as determine if there was a pattern to any of them. A good chart will use symbols to tell you, for example, that not only did you miss your backhand ten times, but you hit eight of them into the net and two wide to the right. From this information, you can then begin to see *why* you might have lost, *where* your errors were, and *what* specifically you need to work on.

It is sometimes difficult to judge from these statistical facts what actually caused or allowed you to play as you did. A "Match Critique Sheet" (page 117) might also help you discover how you performed in the match without listing every won or lost point. This sheet should be filled out by your coach or a qualified but unbiased person watching your match. It lists items such as your concentration and attitude and all of your strokes. Each one is then rated from poor to excellent, and at the bottom of the sheet is a place for a synopsis of your match strengths and weaknesses.

An "Opponent Analysis" (page 116) is another form that you fill out after the match has been played. It lists specific questions about the game of your opponent. It can help you learn more about what took place by learning about his game. This information can help you tremendously should you meet this same person in another match, so it should be kept in a file. What were his weak strokes? What shots can he hurt you with? Is he a slow or fast starter? How would you play and beat him in your next meeting? These and other questions can be found on the form.

If you are unable to recognize these specifics in your opponent's game, you might want to have someone use the "Individual Evaluation Chart" or "Match Critique Sheet" to record your opponent's play during the match. This might enable you to better understand his strengths and weaknesses and help you in filling out the "Opponent Analysis" on him following the match.

These charts and forms are an excellent way to help

you become more aware of what is happening during match play. Not only will you be able to learn more from every match that you play, but after reviewing the forms several times you will begin to be aware of what to look for during the match. You will be able to spot the patterns and trends as they develop in each match. If you are missing a particular shot, or if your opponent is becoming comfortable with a certain stroke, you will learn to be more aware of it when it occurs during a match.

ATTITUDES ARE MORE IMPORTANT THAN FACTS

The fact is that 50% of all players in every tennis match around the world will lose! What shouldn't be so important to you is the fact of winning or losing, but rather that you learn from it and improve.

A loser looks painfully at the facts and wishes he was the winner. He might droop with disgust at his performance for days following an important match. He will make general statements about his play on that particular day, but will rarely pursue the reason for his loss, either in his mind or on the practice court.

Winners, on the other hand, don't live in the past, they learn from it. They look at the facts, but always dig deeper assuming that there is an answer. Their emphasis is not so much on performance as it is on learning. They are open minded, have a positive attitude, and are willing to further themselves in the game. They reason that if they would spend less time dragging around after losses and more time taking positive action to prevent them from happening again, that they'd be all the better for it.

The score at the end of the match is a fact. You may have lost 6-0, 6-1, and these game and set score totals are supposed to represent what took place in the match. Although scores such as this can be hard to take at times, it is what you do *after the fact* that matters most. Understand that although the score is a fact, it really doesn't represent what took place in the match. You might have played a very close match with the score reaching deuce on every game that you lost. This will never be reflected in the score. Analyze what happened at deuce each time to look for the answers to why you may have lost. Maybe it was only a service problem as your normally reliable serve went repeatedly into the net. Instead of being disgusted with your loss, hit the practice court to revive your ailing serve and prevent this from happening again.

Look past the facts for the real answers and strive to learn from them. Any fool can capitalize on his gains and sulk at his losses. It takes players with intelligence to learn from them both.

℞ HOW TO WATCH A MATCH

Tennis is such a fascinating game to watch and can provide a tremendous amount of enjoyment to those who view it being played. When the players involved are of world class ability, the enjoyment is enhanced as the players are so masterful.

The best way to watch a match is not purely for the sake of enjoyment, but rather to benefit from what is taking place. I often encourage my students to watch the professional tournaments on television and local tournament matches to try and understand different players' games and to formulate match strategies. In this way, the time spent watching tennis matches can be used wisely by learning and developing strategies, as well as practicing match awareness.

Start analyzing the tennis matches that you see on television. Picture yourself playing against one of the players and having all the shots and capabilities of a professional yourself. What would be your game plan in order to win? Notice where your imaginary opponent is hitting the ball in different situations. You'll begin to see patterns in his play that can aid you in determining the best game plan to use. Train your mind to look for strengths and weaknesses in others every time you watch a match. You can literally be practicing intelligent play right in your living room studying the players on television!

Matches at your club or local park can also provide this same learning opportunity. Even players you practice with should be sized up according to their strengths and weaknesses. Think about the match play strategies you would use against these players if you were involved in a match with them.

Watching other players hit might also give you insight

into your own strokes. If a particular shot is hit well consistently by someone you are watching, analyze *how* he is doing it. It might give you a better understanding for your own game. Likewise, if he is making errors, try to figure out why to have a clearer picture that could help you with your strokes.

There is much to be learned in watching others play the game of tennis. You can choose to use this time for pure enjoyment, or you can choose to be always improving your own game. Be aware of what is taking place on the court, much as you would if you yourself were playing. You'll be strengthening your mental game as you'll be "practicing" every time you watch a match.

℺ *GET THE MOST FROM YOUR LESSON*

Your tennis game, just like your car, needs a periodic tuneup and check to run properly. When it's time, you should seek the advice of a qualified teaching professional, much the same as you would trust your car to a qualified auto mechanic.

What you get out of your lesson will often depend entirely on you. If you are not properly prepared and in the right frame of mind, you might actually get very little from your lesson. When your concentration and mental focus is not on the present and open for learning, your mind will wander and take in very little. It is your attention span which will determine how much you will learn from each lesson. As a teaching professional, I know that a student will only retain what is being said when his attention span allows him to.

A positive attitude about learning is usually what brings some players along much faster than others in the game. It is an open and willing desire to hear what it is that can help them improve that speeds up the learning process. Others view a lesson as criticism and become defensive or skeptical about adjustments to their game. Their minds are closed to change, and they aren't really in search of a better understanding of their game through a professional eye.

The best way to get the most from your lesson is to be open and prepared to learn. *Ask questions,* if you aren't totally sure of what is being said. A confused mind will always say "No," so ask as many questions as necessary to open

Professional instruction can help to improve your tennis game. What you get out of your lessons will often depend on YOU.

up your mind. You have the right to completely understand what it is your professional is trying to communicate, and to know why he is suggesting the advice.

If you feel you aren't getting what you should out of your lessons, analyze your attitude and attention span during your lesson time. Are you fresh and ready to learn at the beginning of the lesson, arriving in plenty of time to be properly warmed up and ready? Are you asking questions to get a better picture? Are you thinking only of what is being said and what you are doing during the lesson, or is your mind on past or future events? Are you in a good mood and enthusiastic about learning? Are you practicing and working on the new techniques learned?

Often you might find that to get the most from your lesson requires more of a commitment from yourself to learning the game. Being prepared both mentally and physically is of the utmost importance in order to retain and learn the most in the short time span of the lesson. If you find that you are doing the necessary preparation and doing all you can in the lessons, but still aren't benefiting from them, seek the advice of another tennis professional in the form of a second opinion. Patients do this all the time with their doctors, so why shouldn't tennis students. This way you can discover the best advice by seeking the best source. You might even be able to pick up tips from several different professionals to make your own diagnosis. To succeed with a lesson, be open about learning and honest with yourself about your abilities.

I would never attend a lecture and not take notes to help me remember the items of importance. Yet rarely, if ever, do I see tennis students writing down the key points discussed in a tennis lesson. Once these things have been brought out and worked on, it then becomes the student's responsibility to take this professional advice and go and work on it themselves. This is a crucial part of any tennis lesson, the after-practice working on the new techniques. The success of most tennis lessons is decided by the pupil, and what he chooses to do with the advice after it has been shared with him.

⚲ A COMMITMENT

Champions are born in the labor of defeat.

To continue your quest to play your best tennis requires a commitment to learn all that you can about your tennis game. You've got to want it badly enough to make it your purpose to obtain it. Look for all the knowledge that you can use to better your game. Even the pros have "off" days, however, they're the ones who will search for the answers as to why they did.

Have you ever wondered why the professional tour players have coaches they often work and travel with? These players can hit virtually all the strokes in the book, and are where they are because they have proven themselves winners. So why do they need to retain the services of someone to coach them, who most often is less of a player? *They are committed to continue learning! They are great players because they've never stopped learning!*

Watch a match, read a tennis book or magazine, take a lesson, enter a tournament, go out and practice, do whatever is necessary to keep learning more about the game, your game. It will require more effort than doing nothing, but then again, you'll get back what you put into your game. Take a tip from the pros — never stop learning!

⚲ SUMMARY

Be excited about learning more about the game of tennis. The answers to your tennis problems will come out only when you get specific with them. Most players could greatly improve their games if only they knew why they were winning or losing points. There is always a reason for your wins and losses, it just takes intelligence to find the reason and learn from it. Have someone chart your match to help you better understand your own game. Fill out an opponent analysis following your match to better understand your opponent's game. These charts and forms are an excellent way for you to become more aware of what is happening during match play.

Look past the facts to gain the real knowledge of the game, because the score really doesn't give you any specific answers about the match. There is much to be learned in watching others play the game of tennis. You can literally improve your own game just by watching a tennis match intelligently. Be mentally and physically prepared for your lessons. Be open minded, attentive, and ask questions to give yourself the maximum opportunity for improvement during your lessons. Commit yourself never to stop learning about the game of tennis!

Opponent Analysis Form

NAME: _____ OPPONENT: _____

TOURNAMENT: _____ DATE: _____

WON/LOST: _____ ROUND: _____ SCORE: _____

Did he/she prefer to play on the baseline, rush the net or mix it up?

_____

Would you say he/she's an offensive player, a defensive player, or a mixture?

_____

Does he/she hit with topskin, underspin, flat or mixture? _____

Is he/she a patient player or a big hitter? _____

How does he/she handle and react to pressure? _____

Does he/she prefer high or low balls? _____

Does he/she prefer hard or soft balls? _____

Does he/she prefer flat or spin shots? _____

What is his/her favorite shot? _____

What are some of his/her weak strokes? _____

Were you able to play to them? Why or why not? _____

_____

Do his/her service returns float high, stay low, play down the middle or angle wide? _____

How does he/she move (quick, slow, etc.)? _____

Is he/she in shape to last a long match? _____

What shots did he/she hurt you with? _____

What shots did you hurt him/her with? _____

Is he/she a slow starter or a fast starter? _____

Does he/she play better when he's/she's ahead or behind? _____

Was he/she mentally tough? _____

What does he/she tend to do on important points? _____

_____

Is he/she beatable? Why or why not? _____

_____

How will I play and beat him/her in our next meeting? _____

_____
_____
_____
_____
_____
_____

Match Critique Sheet

Name: _____ Date: _____

Tournament: _____ Opponent: _____

Won/Lost: _____ Round: _____ Score: _____

	Excellent	Good	Fair	Poor
Play:				
Concentration	_____	_____	_____	_____
Hustle	_____	_____	_____	_____
Attitude	_____	_____	_____	_____
Strategy	_____	_____	_____	_____
Sportsmanship	_____	_____	_____	_____
Strokes:				
Forehand	_____	_____	_____	_____
Backhand	_____	_____	_____	_____
Volley	_____	_____	_____	_____
Serve	_____	_____	_____	_____
Return of Serve	_____	_____	_____	_____
Overhead	_____	_____	_____	_____
Drop Shot	_____	_____	_____	_____
Approach Shot	_____	_____	_____	_____
Other _____	_____	_____	_____	_____

Your strengths in the match were:

You could use improvement in these areas:

Your own comments on the match:

Individual Evaluation Chart

Name: _____ Date: _____

Tournament: _____ Opponent: _____

Won/Lost: _____ Round: _____ Score: _____

Comments: _____

Symbols

cc = crosscourt	F = Forehand	AS = Approach Shot
dl = down-the-line	B = Backhand	DS = Drop Shot
w = wide	L = Lob	OH = Overhead
l = long	V = Volley	SH = Service Return
n = netted	HV = Half Volley	DF = Double Fault
		SW = Serve Winner

1st set			2nd Set			3rd Set		
Service 1st 2nd	Points	Errors	Service 1st 2nd	Points	Errors	Service 1st 2nd	Points	Errors

CHAPTER 9

Become Your Own Master

⚬ *LEARN TO SEE YOURSELF*

It is no easy task to teach yourself to play the game of tennis. This may be the reason that very few self-taught players have ever achieved great success in the sport. However, whether you want to or not, eventually there are times you will have to be your own tennis coach. In the middle of a match when you need help with your game, who can you turn to? You must be able to turn to yourself!

A tennis teaching professional is expected to be equipped with the proper knowledge of the sport, have the communication skills to give advice in understandable language, but above all, have the perception skills to recognize what aspect of the student's game needs attention. To learn to teach yourself first requires that you see yourself as a teacher might.

To get a better idea of how you play, attempt to become visually aware of your tennis game. Take a look at yourself to see if you are playing the game the way you would like. If you are having a difficult time with this mental picture try to "feel" your style of play by consciously reviewing yourself. *Relax* as you want your strokes to be fluid and natural. Even though you are attempting to better understand your game by seeing yourself, this doesn't mean that you must "think" on your strokes to the point that they appear mechanical. This is often the reason players tighten up as they try to perform their strokes by being too consciously aware of what they are doing.

Have yourself video taped. It's a great way for you to see the way you really play the game.

The best way to clearly see yourself is to have your game videotaped periodically. The old saying "a picture is worth a thousand words" is never truer than it is here. This can help you take a look at your game as a professional might view it. Tape yourself hitting all of your strokes and even playing a match if you can. *Look for details.* Place your hand over your body on the screen and watch only your footwork for a while. Next take a look at your body positioning and balance on your strokes. Are you achieving maximum ball control on each hit? If not, watch the tape over and over again in search of the answer.

Shadow swinging or stroking in front of a mirror can also help you see the way you look hitting a ball. Although these ways aren't as ideal as looking at a videotape, they can offer quick analysis of a problematic stroke.

Seeing yourself is the initial step towards being able to understand what you might be doing. To become your own coach you need to have the eyes of one. Look at yourself objectively as a paid professional would. You can see yourself as well as anyone if only you can learn to open your eyes.

℁ *REALIZE WHAT YOU ARE DOING AND WHY*

So often players are more concerned with the way a stroke *looks* than they are with the *results* of a stroke. They become so stroke conscious, yet they really have no idea what they are doing with the ball. The main concern should always be why the ball goes where it does. The way you look in the stroking process is really only important to how it relates to your control of the ball. If you aren't attuned to this, you will probably lack the necessary awareness of your game to realize what it is that you are actually doing.

Once players learn to realize why the ball goes where it does, they will have a clearer understanding for any stroke correction necessary. To realize what you are doing requires a mind that is observing and sharply aware. Are you just hitting balls or are you watching to see exactly where they go? Do all of your strokes have predetermined targets or just some of them? Do you take the time following an error to assess what happened and to determine why it occurred, or do you just get angry with yourself?

Learn to place less emphasis on *generalities* with your

play. A shot that is judged as being in or out shouldn't be the main concern. Be more specific by watching exactly where the ball is going each time, and seeing if it is going where you intended. If it isn't, this is the time to figure out why it is going where it is. Only when you get specific with your strokes will you be able to learn to correct them yourself.

Realizing what you are doing by always questioning "why" will help you begin to be aware and in tune with your own game. Stay away from hitting balls aimlessly. Every stroke has a target and if the ball doesn't go to the target, there is always a reason. Search for it and you can learn to teach yourself!

THINK ON YOUR OWN

Most of my instructional lessons begin with questioning students about what they would like to work on. Often the reply is, "I don't know." If you truly don't what it is that you need work on, then you probably need to learn how to think for yourself. A tennis professional can think for you during the short span of time in a given lesson, but during the remaining time that you play the game, it becomes imperative that you learn to think for yourself to better understand the strengths and weaknesses of your tennis game.

Going through the motions and being unaware of what you are doing is playing what I call "mindless tennis." Making error after error and watching your game fall apart is senseless; it is playing the game without thinking. A sensible player knows what he is doing, he decides what needs correcting, and he makes the corrections. All this can be done on your own as you play the game. Your mind simply needs to be turned to the "on" position, and you will become the thinking player you want to be!

Players who learn to use their minds are the intelligent ones. They aren't necessarily smarter, they have just learned how to use their minds to get the most out of their games. They turn to themselves when playing a match instead of wondering who to turn to. They play smart tennis because they have learned how to think on their own. Their play usually reflects this fact because they are extremely difficult to beat. You see, thinking players usually won't be the ones who beat themselves!

To think on your own, learn to turn to yourself for the answers. Play the game with your mind turned "on" by being in tune with what is happening. Know what it is that you need to work on, and reason in your mind the corrective action necessary. Play a better game of tennis by simply using good sense and sound judgment with your play.

℺ CORRECT YOUR OWN MISTAKES

Tennis is considered "a game of mistakes" by the majority of players new to the sport. It can be quite a frustrating experience learning to play, but at the same time, it can also present an interesting challenge as you learn to overcome these mistakes and watch yourself improve. Try to enjoy learning what your mistakes are and correcting them, as this is the only way to continue improving your tennis game!

You've probably been correcting a lot of your mistakes all along without even realizing it. Maybe you corrected a stroke while you were out practicing or playing a match, and hit three to four backhands long over the baseline and adjusted your stroke to prevent it from continuing to happen. You recognized your mistake (hitting backhands long) and took corrective action by adjusting your stroke accordingly. You might not have realized exactly how you corrected it, but your backhand didn't continue to go long, so you didn't give another thought to it.

The best preventive medicine for mistakes is a good solid foundation in your understanding of the basics. If errors begin to happen, go back to the basics to analyze and correct them. Analyze your contact and control of the ball. Check to see if you are lining up your body properly. Is your preparation being adjusted to allow for good contact with the ball?

To learn to correct your own errors will require discipline in your judgmental self. Constructive action is needed, not critical advice. This is often the single most difficult thing for players to learn. Observing mistakes non-judgmentally is totally new for most, but is so important in learning to coach yourself.

Conscious corrections of your play can be analyzed in many ways. Check your follow-through to analyze and understand your strokes. Let your ball toss drop and bounce to understand where your toss is going on your serve. Discover where your body weight is shifting by watching to see in which direction you move after you hit the serve. Analyze your intensity to see if you are matching the effort to the task on your strokes.

Over compensation is sometimes one of the best tools for correcting your mistakes. For example, if you are repeatedly netting your serves, attempt instead to hit several long over the service line. Once you have hit a few long serves, try once again to hit them into the net. This way you will find that you are able to get your control back by directing the ball to desired targets. Hopefully, you can find the happy medium that places the ball into the correct service box. If your backhand is going wide to the right each time and you are unable to correct it, try aiming your backhand too far to the left. This overcompensation will help you regain the necessary control over the ball by directing it where you want. Once you have your control back and have hit several balls too far to the left, bring the target back into the court and continue stroking with the desired control. Correcting your own mistakes can help you become a sensible player/coach with consistent results.

ʕ YOU AS YOUR OWN MOTIVATOR

Tennis players often seek the advice of professionals when they find themselves "down" and need to have some part of their game "fixed." The usual lesson includes some degree of positive advice intended to rejuvenate or pick the student back up with motivating thoughts. Although this positive advice is very beneficial, players could progress much faster if only they would learn how to pick themselves up when they find themselves down, and learn to stay motivated on their own.

A good portion of most lessons taught by teaching professionals today is aimed at motivating the student and nurturing confidence. This is a vital part of keeping students on a positive and forward-moving track with their tennis games. Without motivation, players tend to drift without a purpose. Although professionals are a good source of motivational help, they shouldn't be the sole source. When you turn to your pro every time you find yourself "down" and feeling insecure, you will rob yourself of precious lesson time that could be spent more wisely on improving your tennis game. Strive to become your own motivator, to drive yourself, and advance your own game. Believe that you can do it and you will discover that you can!

Pep talks are usually great for initiating short term enthusiasm in yourself, however, to develop self motivation requires a deep desire along with constant thinking of those desires. It must come from within to be strong enough to create an inner fortitude of wanting something badly enough to get it. Someone else might want you to do something and try to motivate you to do it, but unless you feel the inner desire for it yourself and truly believe that you can attain it, there is little hope of achieving it. Tennis parents are a prime example of external motivators trying to instill in their children the same drive and desire that they have for them. Unless they can somehow get the child to become self motivated, all of their efforts will probably be in vain.

Tennis is an individual sport. Such luxuries as organized practices, scrimmages, meetings, coaching, training, etc., that are prevalent in other sports are rare to the average tennis player. In many cases, former athletes in other sports who have taken up tennis are often quite lost as to how to motivate themselves. They've spent the better part of their lives participating in other sports learning to do as they were told and instructed, lacking the necessary self motivation to plan, act, and think for themselves.

Give yourself homework and a plan to guide yourself and your tennis game. Your plan might include a daily regimen to follow, and should be placed somewhere that you will see it often. Setting tennis goals, both short and long term, can also keep your mind focused on the future. Be positive and believe that you can do it by picking yourself up instead of putting yourself down. Become your own motivator and drive yourself to success. Deep desire and belief in yourself will be the motivating force which will take you there.

☿ DON'T EXPECT

Try not to *expect* so much from yourself in learning

the game of tennis. You might anticipate or look forward to seeing your game improve, but you shouldn't expect it to happen immediately. I've learned that as soon as you expect something to happen in life, you'll probably find that you'll be disappointed. If it doesn't happen immediately, you will be unhappy and if it does, you really won't be happy either because you expected it to happen!

Be patient with yourself. Most people I've found are usually much more patient with others than they are with themselves. An effective tennis game also requires a lot of dedication and practice. Success might not occur overnight, and you shouldn't expect it to. Relax yourself, as trying so hard will only cause more tension in your body which will affect the natural flow of your strokes. If things aren't happening with your tennis game at the rate you might like, put forth more positive action in the form of hard work and practice, instead of simply wishing your game would improve. Immediate results in tennis occur very seldom. It is possible, however, to develop an immediate understanding of your game and what you are doing. Once you have developed such an understanding you can recognize and reason things on your own much more easily.

Being your own master means you have the ability to evaluate and coach yourself. This can certainly help expedite the progress of your game as you literally watch yourself during the many hours in practice and match play. Being able to recognize and make changes in your game requires a coach's eye. To make changes in your game and to have them become an automatic part of your play takes a good understanding of what you are doing and, above all, *patience*. Don't expect it all to happen immediately.

ℚ *SUMMARY*

To become your own coach you must first learn to see yourself as a coach might. You can do this as well as anyone if you practice it. Realize *why* the ball goes where it does. Be specific with your strokes in order to correct them yourself. Avoid playing "mindless tennis" by turning your mind "on" and "tuning in" to your game. Players who have learned to think on their own usually won't be the ones beating themselves. Enjoy learning what your mistakes are and correcting them yourself. This can be the quickest way to self improvement as you learn to play a sensible game of tennis. Become your own motivator and "pick yourself up" instead of putting yourself down. You can achieve whatever you want as long as you have an inner desire and belief in yourself. Try not to expect immediate results with your play. To make changes in your game and to have them become an automatic part of your play requires patience and a good understanding of what you are doing.

CHAPTER 10

Practice with Purpose

ℚ *KNOW WHERE YOU'RE GOING*

How will you know when you get there, if you don't even know where you're going?! This is how some tennis players learning to play the game feel. They haven't established their purpose in tennis so they are like a lost ship without a rudder, left to drift in no particular direction. Motivation is what is usually lacking in these players, because they haven't established goals.

If your game is "drifting," take a few minutes to list some tennis goals that you might have. Your goals should be set according to what you want to get out of your game. If it's pleasant exercise or therapy away from other stresses in life that you're after, you might not need to be "goal achieving" since what you are wanting is something more "tension relieving." However, if you are in search of something more than social exercise from your tennis game, you will probably get the most enjoyment from improving your game.

Winning Wimbledon is a popular dream among tennis players, but in order for a dream to become a goal, it should be vivid and repeated often. Frustration won't come from setting a goal and striving for it. It will come from setting unrealistic goals that you'll never reach, and being disenchanted with yourself and your game when you don't achieve them. Players who put themselves down by saying they'll never play Wimbledon are really just saying they haven't set any short-term goals. Their dream of playing

A ball machine can offer the challenge of being the "most consistent partner" for your practices.

Wimbledon is unreachable to them only because they have set no path to take them there. Keep in mind, no matter what your age or level, you will truly only have a chance to play in an event such as Wimbledon if you believe that you can. (Wimbledon has a seniors division, as well as doubles and mixed doubles divisions, so don't count yourself out!)

Having a series of realistic, clearly defined short-term goals will help keep you motivated and bring about a great feeling of accomplishment as you reach each one. A bigger, long-term goal or dream is also great to strive for, but setting realistic short-term goals leading up to it will keep you constantly focused on an attainable achievement.

Place your goals where you can see them and think on them often. You might even want to establish some daily goals for yourself in addition to your short- and long-term ones. Goals should be adjusted and redefined periodically to keep them current and to have them stay clear in your mind. Develop positive thoughts on each of your goals to keep your excitement and enthusiasm enhanced and to remain motivated.

Be patient in your quest of the goals you set. Bill Tilden, one of the greatest tennis players ever, said, "It takes five years to make a tennis player, and ten years to make a champion." Your self motivation and goal-oriented thoughts must be practiced daily. It can be very tedious or you can learn to enjoy it. It just depends on how important being your best is to you.

Tennis, unlike most team sports, is sometimes very lonely. If you don't stay self motivated or goal oriented, it's easy to find yourself slipping. Once you lose the momentum, the desire will be lost also. Know where you are going, and it will become much easier to find the direction to take you there. Remember, it is the players who know where they are going who seem to get there consistently!

ℚ HAVE A PLAN

Every time that you take to the practice court you will be practicing either good habits or bad habits. It is all up to you and how you choose to spend your time. If you are practicing without a plan, chances are you are spending some of your precious practice time developing bad habits.

Plan your practices according to *what* you are practicing for. Is there a tournament coming up or a special match that you need to gear up for? Is there a stroke that needs attention? Maybe you played poorly in your last match and need to correct a part of your game. You might also be playing well, and you simply need to practice to remain sharp. Whatever the case may be, know *what* it is that you are trying to accomplish in the practice in order to plan it properly.

The development of skills in tennis requires persistence and habits. Repetition is what is needed in areas such as stroke, strategy, attitude, consistency, ball control, offensive/defensive play practice, and strength/weakness practice. These particular areas of concern need to be practiced regularly so your confidence in them will remain firm and unwavering.

Plan your practices according to your own needs. Players often practice the way they see others practicing. If your tennis friends or fellow club members aren't practicing correctly, that doesn't mean you have to follow suit. You need to plan your practices according to your own personal needs. If you're unable to find a drill partner to work on your game with you, you might want to use a ball machine, a practice wall, or even take a "hit-with-the-pro" lesson.

Striving for self improvement requires dedication. It is this persistent practice that will improve your game most. Ben McKowen, a top-ranked junior player in the United States for several years during the 1970s, was quite a tennis player except for his second serve. So what did he do to develop it? He dedicated himself to hit second serves *only* all year in tournament play and practice! It took persistence, but he soon developed a second serve to match the rest of his game. It was through this determined effort that he committed to improving the weakest part of his game. He had a plan, and he stuck to it in both practice and match play, and he did it ALL YEAR!

Know what it is that you need to work on, and plan your practices around it. You can improve your game by simply limiting your practice time to allow only for "good habits." Have a plan and commit yourself to it!

℞ *AIMLESS HITTING PRODUCES AIMLESS PLAY*

The biggest way to avoid playing "Intelligent Tennis" is to practice hitting the ball aimlessly. Nothing can bring about negative stroke reinforcement faster than aimless play can.

So many players practice by showing up at the courts just to hit balls. They might do this for an hour or so and then go home with a sense of accomplishment. What they have really been doing is practicing bad habits, negative stroke reinforcement, and poor mental play. They would probably have been better off staying home!

A well-thought out practice might actually require less time and produce more effective results. When every stroke is being hit *deliberately*, there is purpose and meaning behind each shot. Players often attempt to play their matches this way, but forget to practice in the same manner. Serious tournament players have learned the importance of quality practice time. Players wishing to advance their games must also learn to do as the pros do: make their practice time count!

Aimless hitting occurs when players aren't focused on control of the ball. Without a target in mind for each shot, players seem to lose awareness of what they are doing. Concentration is usually a key factor. When the mind starts to wander, so does your control of the ball. Although it might seem that your mind could help you automatically stroke the correct shot, aimless play is usually the result of an unfocused mind. A focused mind could allow you to be in complete control, however.

The best possible practice tool is simply to hit every shot deliberately. Be aware and understand what is happening at all times and practice correcting your ball control should you lose it. Remember that control over the ball ultimately means control over your opponent and the match. Without it, you'll be playing the game aimlessly.

℞ *ALWAYS GIVE 100%*

Practice only when you can give 100% of yourself. If, after analysis of your game, you discover that you are rarely giving that high of a percentage in practice, take a closer look at your attitude.

A good attitude about practice can make the most mundane workout an exciting new day of tennis. It is your desire to improve that sparks your attitude in practice. Parents and coaches alike hate to see a talented player with little desire. Talent is such a terrible thing to see wasted.

Practice intensity to bring yourself to the 100% mark. No ball is *out* in practice, and you should hustle to retrieve *all* balls played to you. In a tennis match, the ball can only bounce once on your side of the court, so *never* let it bounce twice in practice! This intensity and hustle in your play will motivate you to put forth all your efforts to practice your best.

Practicing less than 100% will only cause you to play that way in a match. One of the best ways to commit yourself to play your best tennis is to demand that you never give less than 100% of yourself *every time you step onto the court.* You will discover that your practice time, as well as your match play, will become more exciting and challenging. Your entire attitude can change by learning to give your all every time you play the game!

PRACTICE THE WAY YOU WANT TO PLAY

Practice is the best time to work on your game; to smooth out your strokes and to gain confidence in your play. It is also the ideal time to play "your style" of tennis to be prepared for consistent performances from yourself during match play.

Advanced players realize that it is how you practice that invariably dictates how you will play in a match. If you concentrate, give 100% of yourself, and always have a solid understanding of what you are doing in practice, the transition to match play will be a breeze. On the other hand, if you practice casually, and have a leisurely time hitting a few balls, your adjustment to perform and play at a high standard during match play will be difficult. Your mind and body won't be used to these intense demands, and you will probably have a difficult time keeping your mind on the match and the ball in the court!

Just like everything in life, you'll get back from your tennis game what you put into it. Your practice time is when you should put forth effort into your game. Practice your game the way you want to play it. Stay away from attempting to play the game in your dreams; don't waste your precious time. Play *your* game that you feel comfortable with and that is within your limitations. Allow a high margin for error on all shots just as you would in a match. Going for all of your shots in practice won't help strengthen confidence in your ability, because you'll be making so many unforced errors in the process. You will also find that during match play you will be attempting these same low percentage shots because these are the shots you've been practicing!

If you want to develop part of your game to make it a viable part of your match play, practice is the time to do it. Maybe you've been afraid of the net before, but you've discovered how this could help you become a better player, so you need to practice it. Even though you normally shy away from the net in practice, try to spend as much time at the net as your practice time allows. In this way you'll become accustomed to being there, and as your confidence grows, it will become part of your game.

Play the game of tennis that you want every time you're on the court. Treat practice and match play virtually the same. You'll discover that it will be much easier to play consistent tennis when you have consistent playing habits.

℞ CHALLENGE YOURSELF AGAINST ALL LEVELS

The old adage which says "You won't get better until you practice against better players" isn't true at all. The best way to practice is against players of *all* levels.

Playing a lesser opponent is sometimes even better practice than playing against someone better. Your mind will normally want to wander out of boredom or lack of intensity, and this is an important mental practice lesson to learn. Usually, the weaker the player you are hitting with, the more difficult it will be for you to stay at a peak level of concentration. Take advantage of this opportunity to control the focus of your mind and practice getting mentally tough. If you're playing a practice match, play your best and attempt to win 6-0, 6-0 if you're capable of it. This isn't an easy score to produce, no matter what level your opponent is, and this will help you to keep mentally sharp and give 100%.

Practice especially against players you have a difficult time beating. Maybe they play a game that you just hate to play against. You'll never be able to avoid the problem by running away from it. Face these same players in practice to develop winning strategies against them. You will discover after you've played them several times that they are in fact quite beatable, and the block you've had against them will vanish.

Play against players of your own level in practice also, because they'll often give you a tough match. This can help develop your tenacity and fighting spirit as you must "dig deeper" to win the big points and pull through in the close matches. Playing someone of your own level can also help you practice your stamina and match conditioning. You could be in for a long match if the games prove to be very close.

It seems to be normal that at the club level, players often find a compatible partner and practice with just this person time and again. This is fine if you enjoy playing tennis socially, but if you're trying to improve your game you need to challenge yourself against a variety of players. You must test your mental and physical skills on all types of players in order to have a better understanding of the different game styles in tennis. It's important to expose yourself to a variety of different games, strokes, and styles to be prepared to play well against them all in match situations. Make your practices more challenging by learning to play your best against all levels.

ℚ MASTER THE TIE-BREAKER

Playing tie-breakers in practice can be an effective way to simulate an intense match play situation. All points are considered "big points" in a tie-breaker, and practicing this pressure is an excellent way to develop your confidence in handling it during a real match.

If you've been having a difficult time getting yourself motivated for practice, challenge your practice partner to a best of five or nine tie-breaker series. Every point will then be important to you both, and this should help stimulate your concentration and performance. You will also discover which part of your game needs the most work because invariably, those strokes will be the first ones to go in pressure situations.

When you are serving, each point represents, in effect, an entire service game for you. If you hold or win each one of your service points, theoretically you can't lose in the tie-breaker. This is the same strategy that can be applied to a set when serving: hold all service games in the set and you can't be beaten. This can then be an intense test of your ability to concentrate and make each service point count.

Tie-breakers should be played just as you would in an important match, with a high margin for error on all shots. This is vital in establishing a steady, consistent performance that allows your opponent the chance to make an error first. Practice these big points in a relaxed and confident manner, just as you would like to do in a match.

Your confidence needs to be nurtured in practice. Without it, you'll play a tense, nervous, and rushed game of tennis. When it's present, your play will become smooth, flowing, and controlled. Practice develops confidence in your strokes and play through repetition. It is vitally important for you to believe in yourself and your abilities. Your confidence can be even more strengthened when you become comfortable playing big points and handling pressure situations. Most matches are filled with big points with all the pressure on to perform. The more you practice and feel comfortable playing these big points, the closer you'll get to playing your best tennis.

℘ KNOW WHEN TO STOP

The best thing you could possibly do for yourself when your enthusiasm for practicing is gone is simply to stop practicing! Attempt to revive your attitude and get your mind focused back on the practice if you can, but if it becomes impossible to discipline yourself on a particular day, know when to call it quits!

A player can spend an unlimited amount of time practicing as long as he is practicing *correctly*. Tennis professionals who play the game for a living practice for lengthy periods every day, even while they are competing in tournaments. Although most players realize how important practice is for their games, few realize that incorrect practice can actually hinder their play. Remember that *you must practice correctly* in order to get the benefits derived from practice!

Try to avoid practicing when you have nothing better to do with your time. Practice with a purpose or not at all. As soon as your play becomes sloppy and your concentration is lost, know that it's time to stop. Continuing to practice at this point will only reinforce bad habits in your game, which is not what your practice time is intended for. Don't let yourself continue to practice when you're not practicing well. Discipline yourself to have the desire to work hard, and to take your practices as seriously as you take your matches. Know that it's time to stop when your practice habits turn to bad.

♀ *HOW WELL ARE YOU PRACTICING?*

To help you answer the question of how well you are practicing, you could just as easily ask yourself, "How well have I been playing?" You've probably been playing about as well as you've been practicing!

As you begin the see the correlation between the two, a more important emphasis can then be placed on the way you practice. In order to play intelligent tennis, you must spend your practice time practicing intelligent play. Discipline yourself to practice good habits, to keep your mind focused and your attitude eager. The time spent practicing will then be beneficial to your game and will bring about improvement more quickly.

Try to get more from your practice time. Prepare yourself to practice well, just as you would prepare to play your best during a match. Be mentally and physically ready to give it your best in practice, and chances are you will. If a particular shot isn't working the way you would like, remain at the courts and continue working on it a little longer. Be persistent and know what there is an answer to every problem. Use your practice time wisely to better understand your game.

Be creative to get more out of your practices. I've seen players show up at the courts to practice, and if they couldn't find a partner, go home. Why didn't they go out and practice their serves? The serve is the most important stroke in tennis!

But how much time is really spent practicing this stroke by most players?

The next time you practice, ask yourself, "How well am I practicing?" If you aren't happy with your practice habits, discipline yourself to make practicing more important. Remember, your play is a reflection of your practice.

☿ SUMMARY

List several short- and long-term tennis goals. Think on them often to keep yourself motivated. Know what you are trying to accomplish in your practices in order to plan for them properly. Without a plan, you might find yourself practicing bad habits. Stay away from aimless hitting by having a target in mind for every stroke that you hit. Commit yourself to play your best by giving 100% every time you step onto the tennis court. It is how you practice that will invariably dictate how you play during matches. Learn to treat match play and practice just the same.

Practice against all levels of players. Challenge yourself to play your best no matter what level your practice partner is. Playing tie-breakers in practice is an excellent way to develop your confidence in playing big points and handling pressure. When you lose your enthusiasm for the practice, it's time to stop. You can practice an unlimited amount of time as long as you are practicing correctly. In order to play intelligent tennis, you must spend your practice time practicing intelligent play. You will probably play the game about as well as you have been practicing!

CHAPTER 11

Playing Your Best Consistently

⚘ *THE ULTIMATE MEASURE OF A CHAMPION*

The truly great players in the history of the game have all been consistent performers. Their consistency has been what has made them the champions whose names are in the record books. Players like Bjorn Borg — winning five Wimbledon singles titles; Martina Navratilova — winning the Grand Slam; Rod Laver — winning the Grand Slam of tennis twice; and Roy Emerson — winning more titles than any other player in tennis history.

Why are these players unique? Why can't everyone play well consistently? Most players seem to be on a roller coaster ride with their tennis games because they don't have a clear understanding of how to play *consistent* tennis!

Consistent tennis players are always difficult to beat because they won't beat themselves. They understand that errors are how you win points, so they shy away from taking unnecessary risks with their shots. Senselessly giving away points and making erratic mistakes is not their style. They keep the ball in play with a good margin for error and play an intelligent game of tennis...on a regular basis!

Players who play great one day and poorly the next are the very ones who play the game of tennis "on the edge." Their shots are often aimed at the lines and clear the net by only a fraction. They are the thrill seekers, but rarely the consistent performers.

Your ability to play your best tennis on a regular basis

greatly depends on your level of consistency. Avoid hot/cold play by "feeling" the ball on the strings of your racket, and getting good control over the direction of your shots. Give yourself a good net clearance and stay away from hitting the ball too close to the lines. Play a consistent game of tennis to become the consistent performer you wish to be. Stay away from living your tennis life "on the edge," and you will enjoy consistent play every time you play the game.

♂ *YOU MAKE THE DIFFERENCE*

You are your own "winning edge." You alone make the difference in how you play because only you are in control of it.

You are intended to be the master of your own destiny. Your successes in tennis will come through your efforts and yours alone. You may seek help or knowledge from a coach or friend, but ultimately it will be you who has to take that knowledge and perform with it.

Before looking elsewhere for answers to your game, look to yourself first. Are you in control of the focus of your mind while you're playing? Do you look for excuses when not playing well? Are you taking full responsibility for your own play and the results? Are you thinking for yourself on the court?

Believe in yourself but, above all, be honest with yourself. Know *your* game and its limitations and learn to play within them. Play your game of tennis on a consistent basis to develop the confidence in your play. Think positively about your abilities and above all, stay away from self-defeating thoughts. You can beat yourself simply by thinking you're beaten.

Getting yourself properly prepared can really make all the difference in your play. Be ready to play your best by practicing correctly, getting mentally and physically in shape, learning all you can, and finding a routine that you feel comfortable with.

Turn your mind "on" when playing and learn to think for yourself. You can make all the difference in your play if you turn to yourself for the answers more often. If you want to be a consistent performer, simply act and play like one. You can do it because you're in control of it!

℺ *CALM CONFIDENCE*

Although giving 100% effort is ideal, *trying* too hard isn't the way to play your best tennis. Trying will only tense muscles and prohibit smooth and flowing strokes. Instead of trying so hard to play your best, simply relax and believe, and you will discover that you will be playing your best more often.

Your balance, coordination, and control all require relaxed muscles in order to be most effective. Your mind also works best when it is calm, free from internal and external distractions. When your mind is calm and your body is relaxed, tennis becomes an effortless game.

Winners believe they will win until the final point of the match has been played. They see clear images and are in control of their thoughts. They play the game as if they were unable to lose. They believe in themselves strongly because they have blocked out all negative and self-defeating thoughts. They see what they want to happen, not fear what might happen.

The mind of a winner is "quiet." It is at ease because it is disciplined and highly concentrated. A winner needn't think on his strokes, he just believes in them and lets his mind control his play. He plays the game in automatic because he has the calm confidence in his abilities and himself.

℺ *THE WINNING ATTITUDE*

Your attitude can help you become a better player overnight! Nothing can help your game more than a positive attitude and an enthusiasm for what you are doing. Since an attitude is formed by habits of thought, yours can be shaped through discipline over what you are thinking.

Your tennis future is decided by what you think and believe. Think discouraging thoughts and you will be a discouraged tennis player. Think encouraging thoughts and you will be an encouraged and motivated player. Your mind responds to your feelings and thoughts. What you think about most often will probably form your attitude. Control what you let yourself think in order to develop your attitude into whatever you desire it to be.

The most determined player is usually the winner. It is their "gutsy" attitude that pulls them through when matches become close. They give 100% effort in a focused way, and reach their peak consistently. They play their best tennis because they're intense, aware, and totally into the match.

A winning attitude doesn't mean that you should be obsessed with WINNING. Quite the contrary. The best attitude is not one of striving for winning, but rather striving for your best play. Don't live in the past with your game, learn from it. Go forward in a positive way and with a winning attitude.

⚲ CONSISTENT HABITS BRING CONSISTENT PLAY

Discipline is a very important prerequisite to playing consistently well day after day. A commitment to constantly work at playing your best is required to achieve it.

Your habits are your usual manner of behavior and conduct. Habit patterns though can be changed by simply changing your thoughts and actions into those you desire. To achieve consistent results with your tennis game, your behavior and conduct on the tennis court should also be consistent. It is this regularity that produces consistent habits as well as consistent performance on the tennis court.

Keep yourself motivated by frequently thinking on an attainable achievement. Players who have concentration and intensity problems need to keep themselves "up" by rededicating themselves to their tennis goals more often. This mental discipline can help to develop good positive habits of thought.

Strive to play the same game of tennis every time you hit. This is not to get your game into a rut, rather it's to practice similar play to develop a consistent game. Tennis players who have a different game every time they hit are apt to have fluctuating results with their play. They haven't learned how to perform on a consistent basis, because their habits are too varied. Develop consistent habits if you desire consistent play.

⚲ HOW IMPORTANT IS YOUR TENNIS TO YOU?

What priority is tennis in your life? Take a moment to

think about your priorities and see where tennis fits in. If you have many other interests and responsibilities in life, you may find that tennis isn't really as important to you as you thought. This is extremely important to realize, so that you can put your game into proper perspective.

Top-ranked players almost always place tennis as the number one priority in their lives. They live, eat, and sleep tennis because it's what is always on their minds. Now, I'm not saying that you should make tennis number one in *your* life — that decision has to come from you alone. I simply think you should realize where tennis is in your realm of importance compared to the players you want to emulate. Are you willing to give up everything to make tennis first in your life like they have?

Don't be upset with yourself if you don't always play your best tennis if tennis is at a lower level on your priority list. If, however, you would like to improve your play, think about making tennis more important to you. Think on your game often when you're not playing. Keep yourself enthusiastic and excited about tennis by reading tennis books or magazines, and watching and playing the game more often. Block out less important things in your life, and refocus your thoughts on tennis. Commit yourself to your tennis game if you would like to improve. But, above all, remember to be compassionate with yourself and your game if tennis is not one of the most important things in your life.

⚲ *SENSIBLE PLAY*

Players who have good "court sense" appear to be in the right place at the right time when they play. Their court coverage seems to be superior because they remember previous situations and are alert to them when they occur again. They anticipate what shots their opponent will hit by reading their opponent and perceiving where the shot he hits will go.

A sensible tennis player is best described as one in control. He is in control of himself, the ball, his opponent, and the match. The game he plays looks easy because it is smooth and effortless. Rarely will his strokes ever look rushed or hectic because he understands that it takes a controlled swing to hit a controlled ball. Sensible players make mistakes, but rarely will they repeat these mistakes over and over. They are aware of what they are doing, and constantly make conscious adjustments to their game. They know their limitations and play their game within them. They have good feeling on their shots because of their solid understanding and application of the basics. Flashy play isn't a sensible player's idea of good tennis. They are usually unconcerned with the way they look because they are so interested in the results of their play.

Your mind has the ability to be sharp and aware of what you are doing on the tennis court if you learn to block out interfering thoughts. Keep your mind in the *now* and concentrate your efforts on your attention. Play the game the way you want, in control and confident. Use your mind to avoid playing a "mindless" game of tennis filled with dumb mistakes. Play the percentages and the odds are in your favor that your sensible play will help you become a consistent performer.

ENJOY WHAT YOU ARE DOING

When you stop having fun playing tennis, you will probably stop playing well. It's important always to have fun, to feel good, and to enjoy playing the game. If you're not enjoying what you're doing, how do you expect to do it well?

Once your enthusiasm for the sport is gone, nothing will come easily. Just like other things in life that become difficult once you determine you don't like them, tennis becomes a much tougher sport to master when you don't enjoy playing it.

Enthusiasm is a powerful driving force within you. Use it to spark your enjoyment of the game. Block out all negative and discouraging thoughts that defeat the enthusiasm you have for tennis. Tennis is a wonderful game and there are few enjoyments better than playing some of the best tennis that you're capable of!

You will achieve nothing great in tennis if you have no enthusiasm for it. However, with the enthusiasm, you can achieve anything you desire! Enjoy learning all you can about the game and strive to become a dedicated student in the process. You will become as good a player as you let yourself be.

ꝗ SUMMARY

Your ability to play your best tennis on a regular basis depends on your level of consistency. Your successes in tennis will come through your efforts alone. Learn to trust in yourself for the answers. Relax and believe, and you will find that you're able to play the game in automatic more often. A winner's mind is quiet...he doesn't have to think on his strokes, he just believes in them! Change your attitude into a positive one and become a better player overnight. It takes discipline to be able to play consistently well day after day. Make your habits as consistent as you want your play to be. Commit yourself to improving your tennis game because you've made it important in your life. Play a sensible game of tennis on a regular basis to become a consistent performer. *Enjoy playing the game of tennis.* You'll never know how good you can actually be until you do!

Skip serving.

ABOUT THE AUTHOR

Skip Singleton is the Director of Tennis at Bluewater Bay Resort in Niceville, Florida. Bluewater Bay was selected by the Florida Tennis Association as "Tennis Club of the Year" for 1986-87 and 1988-89 and is a Five Star Rated Tennis Resort by *World Tennis Magazine*. Skip has received the highest rating of certified teaching professionals by the United States Professional Tennis Association and was named "Professional of the Year" by the USPTA Florida Division for 1989. He has held state and national rankings since he was a junior and has competed on professional circuits in the U.S. and Europe. He has worked both on and off the court with internationally known and respected coaches and players. Skip is involved in many aspects of the tennis industry and is currently an officer on the USPTA Florida Board, tournament director for the largest professional tennis event in northwest Florida, an active speaker nationally, and member of the Prince Teaching Professional Advisory Staff. Skip lives with his wife, Debbie, and dogs, Ace and Volley, at Bluewater Bay Resort in Niceville, Florida.

⚲ ABOUT KEN ROSEWALL

Born in Sydney, Australia on November 2, 1934, Ken Rosewall works on his tennis with the discipline and intensity which have kept him a winner since 1952. As a 19-year-old in 1953, Ken won the first of four Australian championships, the youngest player ever to take that title. He won the Australian for the last time in 1972, 19 years after his first win. He became the youngest French champion in 1953 and repeated the win 15 years later in 1968. He was the U.S. amateurr champion in 1956, and 14 years later in 1970, won the U.S. Open at Forest Hills. Although he reached the finals four times over a 10-year stretch, Wimbledon is he only major title which has eluded Rosewall. In 1971, the Queen awarded him the Order of the British Empire as a consolation prize. Rosewall has said of himself, "Probably the biggest reason I've lasted so long is that I learned the game the right way." Rosewall still resides in Sydney, Australia.

ABOUT LEROY NEIMAN

LeRoy Neiman's art chronicles man at his leisure, not only sporting events, but Las Vegas, Fashion, the Opera, the Theater, Bars, Cars, and Resorts. All that glitters in present day American culture is colorfully rendered by Neiman's brush and pen. He is a superb draftsman and in addition, a brilliant colorist. Yet his art transcends his technical skill. He catches the moment and mood that is the essence of an event or happening. And his art seldom fails to evoke a response in the viewer such as — yes, that picture is the embodiment of the expectancy, color, and excitement of a critical point in a tennis match.

Index